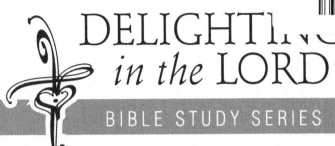

DELIGHTING in the LORD

BIBLE STUDY SERIES

DELIGHTING IN A LIFE OF TRIUMPH

A study on the life of Joseph from Genesis 37-50

by Stacy Davis and Brenda Harris

A Ministry of Calvary Chapel Chester Springs Women in Christ

Delighting in a Life of Triumph
A Study on the Life of Joseph from Genesis 37-50
Part of the Delighting in the Lord Bible Study Series

© Copyright 2018
Calvary Chapel Chester Springs
PO Box 595, Eagle, PA 19480

ISBN 9781723283345

Series Cover Design: Melissa Bereda
Cover Photo: Pexels

Printed in the United States of America

"The one thing I ask of the Lord - the thing I seek most - is to live in the house of the Lord all the days of my life, delighting in the Lord's perfections and meditating in his temple." Psalm 27:4

DELIGHTING
in the LORD
BIBLE STUDY SERIES

CONTENTS

DELIGHTING IN A LIFE OF TRIUMPH

A Study on the Life of Joseph from Genesis 37-50

"But as for you, you meant evil against me;
but God meant it for good,
in order to bring it about as it is this day,
to save many people alive."
Genesis 50:20

ACKNOWLEDGMENTS

"There are diversities of gifts, but the same Spirit.
There are differences of ministries, but the same Lord.
And there are diversities of activities but it is the same God who works all in all.
But the manifestation of the Spirit is given to each one for the profit of all."
1 Corinthians 12:4-7

Many people with different gifts have come together for the common purpose of sharing God's Word (Matthew 28:19-20). This study is the product of those people and their gifts working together by God's grace. We are so thankful for each person and the role they fill.

Pastor Chris Swansen - Theological Editor, Calvary Chapel Chester Springs
Pastor Steven Dorr - Pastoral Support, Calvary Chapel Chester Springs
Carinna LaRocco - Copy Editor
Joan Purdy - Copy Editor
Melissa Bereda - Graphic Designer
Lynn Jensen - Administrative Support

A huge thank you, as well, to the families that allow us to use their second homes for writing getaways.

Additionally, we could not fulfill this calling without the love and support of our husbands and children. From the time God called us to write women's Bible studies, we have considered the call "our reasonable act of service" (Romans 12:1) to Him. Our families and those involved in the DITL ministry join us in this calling. We pray that these studies will be used by God to draw many deeper into His Word and to the heart of God so that lives and relationships will be transformed by His great power and grace.

With love in Christ,
Stacy and Brenda
Delighting in the Lord Ministry

ABOUT THE DELIGHTING IN THE LORD MINISTRY

In 2006, with the Lord's call and leading, Stacy Davis began teaching a Thursday morning Bible study for women at her home church, Calvary Chapel Chester Springs. Each Thursday the ladies met for Bible teaching and small group discussion. In 2008, Stacy asked Brenda Harris to pray about joining the Thursday Bible study as a small group leader. That year, Stacy also asked each small group leader to teach one of the weekly sessions. It was then that Stacy and Brenda's ministry relationship began. The following year, Stacy asked Brenda to pray about joining the teaching team full-time. Prior to serving in this capacity, Brenda answered God's call years before to "make fishers of men" (Matthew 4:19) as God opened doors for a speaking ministry in other churches. Now God would be using Brenda's gift of teaching in her home church. Unbeknownst to them, God was doing a much larger work as He was laying the groundwork for the Delighting in the Lord ministry.

For the next two years, Stacy and Brenda taught the women who gathered on Thursday mornings using Bible study materials from other Calvary Chapel churches and authors. In 2010, Stacy was diagnosed with invasive breast cancer and Brenda jumped in to be more hands-on in women's ministry. It was during that year that God planted the writing seeds in Stacy's and Brenda's hearts. Sensing the Lord's direction to study the book of Matthew the following year, Stacy and Brenda searched for a women's Bible study on Matthew and found nothing that covered the whole book in a verse-by-verse format, with emphasis on life applications. As Stacy prayed seeking God's direction, God continued speaking to her heart, telling her to "write the study." With much fear and trepidation, Stacy shared this with Brenda who then also began diligently praying for God's direction. As Brenda sought the Lord, He gave her the READ format vision, and then He gave them both Psalm 27:4 which became their ministry verse and foundation:

"The one thing I ask of the Lord, the thing I seek most, is to live in the house of the Lord all my life, *delighting in the Lord's* perfections, and meditating in His temple" (NLT).

After much prayer and with the faith to believe that, if God called them, He would equip them, the **Delighting in the Lord Bible Study Series** was birthed that year.

2011 was spent studying and writing "Delighting in the King," a women's Bible study on the book of Matthew. God brought many to support the work including: Pastor Chris Swansen, who read every page of the study for Biblical accuracy; a group of ladies who were grammatical editors; and a fabulous graphic designer, Melissa Bereda. She designed, and continues to design, all the logos, covers, and interior pages, as she too answered God's call on her life to use her gifts for God's glory.

That year, upon suggestion from the ladies, the Thursday morning teaching sessions were video recorded and the church began putting all the materials online. Since then, God has used Stacy and Brenda to bring forth His Word, both in written and spoken form, to the women attending the weekly study. What began as a simple "Yes, God" became a ministry that teaches God's Word to women, drawing out His truths and life applications. They are simply two women who love Jesus with their whole hearts and lives. They have experienced the power of the cross in their own lives and want to tell others of the saving power and grace of Jesus, so others can live a life of peace and joy in the midst of life's chaos. Even more, so that others can live with hope, knowing their eternal home with Jesus awaits. Since its beginnings in 2011, Stacy and Brenda have written 10 verse-by-verse Bible studies for women. They are humbled hearing testimonies of God's transforming work of the Holy Spirit as women have used these studies to delve into God's word.

ADDITIONAL STUDIES IN THE
DELIGHTING IN THE LORD BIBLE STUDY SERIES

Each verse-by-verse study is inductive and deductive with
life application emphasis following the **READ** format:
Receive God's word, **Experience** God's word,
Act on God's word, **Delight** in God's word.

Delighting in the King: Matthew (*currently being revised*)

Delighting in God, His Righteousness and Perfect Plan: Romans

Delighting in Being a Child of God: 1,2 & 3 John

Delighting in God's Will and His Provision: Jonah & Nahum

Delighting in the Redeemer, a Love Story: Ruth

Delighting in God's Heart: A study on the Life of David through
1 & 2 Samuel and the Psalms

Delighting in The Holy Spirit: Acts

Delighting in Being a Woman of God: Esther

Delighting in a Life Lived for God: 1 Peter

All studies are available at www.DelightingintheLord.com

DELIGHTING
in the LORD
BIBLE STUDY SERIES

ABOUT THE AUTHORS

STACY DAVIS has been teaching women God's Word for over 15 years. She has learned many Biblical truths through difficult trials. Beginning at the age of three with her mother's brain aneurism, to the death of her fourth son and through invasive breast cancer, Stacy's faith has been tried and tested many times over. Her life gives testimony to God's redeeming and transforming power. Stacy teaches with passion the truths of God's Word, desiring to share with all women how to go through everyday struggles victoriously in Jesus Christ. She lives in PA with her husband, Barclay. They have six children.

BRENDA HARRIS's background in education, along with her many years as a classroom teacher, was foundational for the plans God had for her to serve Him. In 2006, she transitioned away from instructing young people how to read literature, and began teaching women they can have a closer walk with the Lord through reading and studying their Bible. She is an enthusiastic teacher who loves a great visual to help demonstrate practical ways to apply God's Word to real life. Brenda lives in PA with her husband, Michael, and their two children.

DELIGHTING in the LORD
BIBLE STUDY SERIES

INTRODUCTION

DELIGHTING IN A LIFE OF TRIUMPH

The Life of Joseph from Genesis 37-50

*"Genesis is a book about the beginning of many things:
the world, man, sin, civilization, the nations, and Israel."*
(The KJV Ryrie Study Bible)

Genesis is the very first book of the Bible. Within its pages there are many firsts which take place: the creation of the world, man's original sin, the great flood, and God's covenant with mankind. It is a book which records historical events, but it also contains biographies of the very first people who inhabited the earth including: Adam, Eve, Noah, Abraham, Isaac, Jacob, and Joseph. Genesis was written to understand who we are and how we got here. It is believed Moses was the author, and he chronicled the events in order to have a permanent document of what had occurred in previous generations.

In this study we will be examining only Genesis chapters 37-50 (excluding 38), which describe the life of Joseph. Although Joseph was Jacob's eleventh son, he was Rachel's long awaited firstborn. His name means "God adds." He was the favored son of Jacob, and the obvious display of favoritism caused a great division between Joseph and his brothers. He will endure much because of the favoritism of his father. But despite all that Joseph would endure over his 110-year lifespan, he demonstrates many of Christ's attributes. Joseph, like Jesus, was mistreated, put in prison, rescued others from death, and extended unmerited forgiveness. As Joseph will be used by God to save a nation, his life, in many ways, mirrors what Christ would do for humanity in saving us. Throughout our study we will point out these attributes and similarities, along with others that make Joseph a type of Christ.

Joseph is a story of triumph amidst tragedy. By God's providence, he is a victor; not a victim. There is much to learn from him, and it is our prayer that, as you explore the richness of this story with us, you will grow closer to God and experience your own triumphs in Christ.

AUTHOR

Moses

AUDIENCE

The Israelites

DATE

No one knows for sure, however, Moses may have lived from 1527 BC - 1407 BC. Therefore the book would have been written in that time frame.

WEEKLY WRITTEN LESSONS

This study on the life of Joseph has been broken into nine weeks. Each week there is only one "day" of homework, which means that you will go through the R.E.A.D. format once a week. There will be one or two "Experience" sections for each week. In this section, you will read the verses and answer questions from the text. After you go through the text, you will move on to the application section called "Acting on God's Word." Here you will apply what you've learned to your own life. This is such a necessary step, so be sure to take the time to consider how God is speaking to your heart and life. The last section is your time to reflect and delight in God and what He has taught you. We will ask you to end with a verse that God spoke to your heart that week. This would be a great verse to memorize.

You may choose to do your homework in one sitting or in many; it is totally up to you. You should plan on about 60-90 minutes to complete each week's study. We highly encourage you to spend the time in God's Word answering these questions and digging into the text for yourself. You will find that your time investment will be given back to you deeply for your spiritual growth.

DELIGHTING in the LORD
BIBLE STUDY SERIES

FORMAT: "READ" THE BIBLE

*The format for this study follows the acronym **READ**: Read the Bible.*

RECEIVING God's Word

1. **Open in Prayer:** Before reading God's word, you need to prepare your heart to receive from Him what He has for you.
   • During this time of prayer, confess any sin that may be present in your life.
   • Ask God to open "the eyes of your heart" (Eph 1:18) so you can hear from Him what He wants to communicate to you.
   • Thank Him in advance for what He will do!
2. Receiving: Read the scripture text given.

EXPERIENCING God's Word

This is where you will dive into the Bible and the daily chapter/verses. You'll be answering questions that lead you through the text by first observing the details, and then focusing on the connections within the text to the bigger picture. At other times, you may be investigating other verses from the whole counsel of God, and then drawing some Biblical conclusions from what you have read. There may be several "experiences" drawn from the text.

ACTING on God's Word

In this part of the study you will be applying these verses to your life. We read in Hebrews 4:12 that God's word is "living and powerful, and sharper than any two-edged sword, piercing even to the division of soul and spirit, and of joints and marrow, and is a discerner of the thoughts and intents of the heart." Therefore, as you are studying, God will be speaking to your heart and life. We will be encouraging you to look at applications, but God may have other things He is speaking to your heart. We pray you hear directly from Him. As you listen to the Lord speak to your heart, may He show you what steps He desires you take as you walk out your faith in Him.

DELIGHTING in God's Word

In this final section you will reflect upon what you have learned and offer up your praise and thanksgiving to the Lord. As you close out your daily time, may you truly find that He is the delight of your heart! He fills like no other and nothing else can. And as you "delight yourself in the LORD" He will give you the desires of your heart (Psalm 37:4); because after studying His word, your desires and His should be the same. Through your time in God's word, may you grow more and more into His image. You will be asked to record a verse (or as many as you want!) that stood out to you from the text, and then memorize it if you so desire.

DELIGHTING IN MY SALVATION

If you have never accepted Jesus Christ as your Savior but desire to take that step of faith, all you need to do is:

Recognize that God loves you!

"For God so loved the world that He gave His only begotten Son, that whoever believes in Him should not perish but have everlasting life." (John 3:16)

"But God demonstrates His own love toward us, in that while we were still sinners, Christ died for us." (Romans 5:8)

Admit that you are a sinner.

"For all have sinned and fall short of the glory of God." (Romans 3:23)

"As it is written: 'There is none righteous, no, not one;' " (Romans 3:10)

Recognize Jesus Christ as being God's only remedy for sin.

"For the wages of sin is death, but the gift of God is eternal life in Christ Jesus our Lord." (Romans 6:23)

"But as many as received Him, to them He gave the right to become children of God, to those who believe in His name:" (John 1:12)

"For I delivered to you first of all that which I also received: that Christ died for our sins according to the Scriptures, and that He was buried, and that He rose again the third day according to the Scriptures." (1 Corinthians 15:3, 4)

Receive Jesus Christ as your personal Savior!

"If you confess with your mouth the Lord Jesus and believe in your heart that God has raised Him from the dead, you will be saved." (Romans 10:9)

Prayer is simply "talking with God." Right now, go to God in prayer and ask Christ to be your Savior. You might pray something like this:

"Lord Jesus, I need You. I confess that I am a sinner and that You paid the penalty for my sin through Your death on the cross. I believe that You died for my sins and were raised from the dead. I ask You to come into my heart, take control of my life, and make me the kind of person that You want me to be. Thank You for coming into my life as You promised." Amen.

If you have prayed to accept Christ as your Savior, please tell someone today! Share this exciting news with a close Christian friend, your small group leader or your pastor. They will be thrilled to encourage you in your faith and your decision to follow Jesus!

WEEK 1

TRIUMPH OVER BITTERNESS

Genesis 37

It was the Sabbath and many were making their way to the Synagogue. Jesus was among the crowd when he encountered a man with an afflicted and disfigured hand. Moved with compassion, Jesus called this man forward from the crowd. The Pharisees and Sadducees who stood in the crowd looked intently on Jesus, anxiously waiting to see what He would do. Jesus knew their hearts and the hardness therein; hearts tied up in envy, pride, bitterness and anger. He was jeopardizing their very position as the religious elite and their power over the people. Jesus knew they were watching. After probing into the hearts of the onlookers and exposing what was there, He healed the sick man's hand. The Pharisees were enraged. How dare Jesus heal on the Sabbath, going against "their law" and man-made traditions! How dare He make a spectacle of them and under-mine their authority as the religious elite! Their power, position, and influence was teetering in the balance. We are told in Matthew 12:14, "The Pharisees went out and plotted against Him, how they might destroy Him." As we will see today, bitterness in the hearts of the religious elite during Jesus' day echoes of sin in previous generations as "nothing is new under the sun" (Ecclesiastes 1:9).

We are going back in time to Genesis 37 and meeting Joseph whose life we are studying. He was the first of two sons born to Jacob and Rachel, and he had ten older half brothers. Joseph was loved deeply by his father who openly esteemed him among his brothers. His position was one that his brothers envied. It bred jealousy and a sense of entitlement to power that angered them. Who was Joseph to take what was theirs, especially from Rueben, the firstborn? Just as Jacob stole Esau's birthright years before by receiving his father's blessing, history would now be repeated in Jacob's own sons. We will see the older brothers' bitterness breed envy, anger and ultimately violence against Joseph as they cast him into a pit, sell him to the Gentiles, and then watch him be carried off to Egypt as a slave.

Just as we saw the religious elite embittered toward Jesus, so too, we will see Joseph's brothers embittered toward Joseph. As we study Scripture, we often see types of Christ revealed. Through Joseph's life, we will find a type of Christ repeated through Genesis 37-50. Joseph shines forth from the pages of Scripture as practically flawless. We know he wasn't, but God chose not to speak of those flaws, instead God emphasized his steadfast faith and godliness.

James Montgomery Boice says this regarding the life of Joseph, "Thus begins one of the remarkable life stories of the Bible and all literature. [Joseph] He was loved and hated, favored and abused, tempted and trusted, exalted and abased. Yet at no point in the one-hundred-and-ten-year life of Joseph did he ever seem to get his eyes off God or cease to trust him. Adversity did not harden his character. Prosperity did not ruin him. He was the same in private as in public. He was a truly great man."

It has often been said that bitterness is a poison we drink every day hoping the other person will die. Instead, it slowly kills us by creeping into relationships, attitudes and responses. It is ugly. But take heart, God has the remedy for bitterness, and we will see throughout our study that the evil meant by Satan to destroy can be used by God for His eternal good and glory. Brenda and I, Stacy, pray God will use this study to heal your broken relationships, restore fellowship, and increase your faith in Jesus Christ.

RECEIVING God's Word

Open in Prayer
Read Genesis 37:1-36

EXPERIENCING God's Word

Experience 1: Genesis 37:1-11

1. Read Genesis 37:1-2. In these verses we learn about Jacob (also known as Israel) and his father, Isaac. We are told in verse 1 that Jacob lived in the land of Canaan where his father was a stranger. Isaac's father was Abraham (Abram) and he also was a stranger in this land.

   a. Read Genesis 12:1-7. What command and what promise was given to Abram from God that involved Canaan and Abram's descendants?

b. Read Genesis 17:1-8. Why is it significant that Jacob is living in the land where his father and grandfather were strangers?

2. In Genesis 37:2 we are introduced to Joseph who is one of Jacob's twelve sons. Read Genesis 35:22-26 and fill in the names next to the bullet points below to understand the family genealogy of Abraham.

Abraham – married Sarah (Genesis 11:29)
Isaac – married Rebekah (Genesis 24:67)
Isaac and Rebekah had two sons — Esau and Jacob (Genesis 25:24-26)

Jacob married Leah and they had six sons. List their names:

-
-
-
-
-
-

Jacob also married Rachel and they had two sons. List their names:

-
-

Jacob had relations with Bilhah (Rachel's maidservant) and they had two sons. List their names:

-
-

Jacob had relations with Zilpah (Leah's maidservant) and they had two sons.

List their names:

-

-

3. Read Genesis 37:2-4. Joseph is 17 years old and went out to the field with his half brothers to take care of the flock. Joseph observed something about their behavior and told his dad.

   a. From these verses, what are we told about Jacob's (Israel) relationship with Joseph?

   b. How does Jacob make his affections and partiality known publicly regarding Joseph?

   c. What effect does Jacob's affections and Joseph's behavior have on the half brothers? In answering this question, consider the biological family line of Jacob, his multiple wives/maidservants and his many children.

4. Read Genesis 37:5-8. Describe Joseph's dream and the impact it had on his older brothers. How did they respond?

    a. This dream will be significant as we move through the life of Joseph. Consider the specifics of the dream and the symbolism.

5. Read Genesis 37:9-10. Joseph has a second dream and shares it with his brothers and father. Describe the dream.

6. Read Genesis 37:11. Describe the response of the father and the brothers.

Experience 2: Genesis 37:12-36

1. Read Genesis 37:12-14. Jacob is curious about his sons who are out tending sheep in Shechem, which is about 40 miles away. Jacob sends Joseph to check on his brothers. Why is this a curious command given the known family dynamics?

   a. What do you notice about Joseph's response to his father's request?

2. Read Genesis 37:15-17. Joseph travels to find his brothers but cannot locate them in Shechem. From these verses, how do you see God ordering Joseph's steps?

3. Read Genesis 37:18-24 and answer the following questions:

   a. What do the brothers call Joseph when they see him approaching?

   b. What action verbs are used to describe the brothers' evil plan for Joseph?

c. Reuben, the firstborn in the family, comes to Joseph's defense. Reuben appears to assert his position as the family heir sensing it might be in jeopardy. Read Genesis 35:22. What did he do to try and secure his birthright?

d. In verses 18-22 Reuben tries to alter the evil plot. What is his motive and how might this benefit him and his position within the family?

e. What did the brothers ultimately do with Joseph?

4. Read Proverbs 6:12-19.

a. How is a worthless person described?

b. What are the things God hates according to these verses?

c. How do the brothers demonstrate some of these attributes toward Joseph?

5. Contrast Joseph's situation in Genesis 37:24 with his brothers' position in Genesis 37:25.

   a. Read Genesis 42:21. What additional details do you learn in this verse about Joseph's emotional state when in the empty pit?

6. Read Genesis 37:25-28 and answer the following questions:

   a. Judah intercedes on Joseph's behalf. There seems to be two motives at play in these verses. Describe the possible motives.

   b. What do the brothers do with Joseph and where is he going?

   c. How were the Ishmaelites a way of escape for Joseph but temptation for Joseph's brothers?

> Ishmaelites were descendants by Abraham and Hagar (Gen 16:15) and the Midianites (Gen 37:28) descended from Abraham by his concubine Keturah (Gen 25:2). The term Ishmaelite became a general designation for desert tribes, so that Midianite traders were also known as Ishmaelites. (*Bible Knowledge Commentary*, Old Testament, p. 88)

7. Read Genesis 37:29-31. It appears that Reuben was absent from the decision to sell Joseph. When he realizes what they have done, he rips his clothes as a sign of grief. What realization does Reuben have regarding the actions of his brothers and how it will affect him?

8. Read Jeremiah 9:3 and Genesis 37:31-35. How do you see the snowball effect of sin at work in these verses?

9. The chapter ends in Genesis 37:36 by describing Joseph's new position in Potiphar's house. Contrast how Joseph's position has changed from the beginning to the end of the chapter.

   a. How do you see the sovereignty of God at work in the life of Joseph to this point?

TIME STAMP

Before the digital age, when important paper documents were received, a clerk would use an ink stamp to mark the time and date on them to stand as an official record of an event. It has been said that life events can also be like "time stamps" upon our hearts. Incidents that happen in life, both good and bad, leave an indelible stamp upon us and are not easily forgotten.

Joseph has many "time stamp" moments in his life. As you look back on this week's lesson, what events would you say are "time stamp" moments for Joseph?

A ACTING on God's Word

"Pursue peace with all people, and holiness, without which no one will see the Lord:
looking carefully lest anyone fall short of the grace of God;
lest any root of bitterness springing up cause trouble, and by this many become defiled."
Hebrews 12:14-15

"Root of bitterness." What an interesting analogy used in the book of Hebrews to describe how bitterness can be a hidden emotion, much like the roots of a plant are hidden in the soil. Bitterness, when allowed to fester, becomes like a poison to the spiritual growth of a person. It can grow rapidly and becomes toxic to overall health. Further, bitterness can be a hidden sin which fosters sarcasm, passive-aggressive behaviors and careless words. As the root of bitterness grows a stronger and thicker root system, other sins branch from it. Those sins can quickly escalate into highly detrimental behaviors that may eventually be witnessed outwardly as anger, retaliation, unforgiveness and violence.

Based on our text today I, Brenda, believe it is safe to say Joseph's brothers had a root of bitterness toward Joseph. They hated him (Gen 37: verses 4 & 8), could not speak peaceably with him (v4), envied him (v11), and were sarcastic (v19). These were observable sins and the precursors to their eventual desire to kill him (v20). Each person played a part in the unhealthy interactions in chapter 37. Sin rarely takes only one person down. Sin has a nasty and predictable pattern. When sin is left unchecked, it eventually leads to death as James 1:15 tells us, "Then, when desire has conceived, it gives birth to sin; and sin, when it is full-grown, brings forth death." It is vital we recognize bitterness when it is being conceived in our hearts and then cut it off at the root.

1. How could Joseph, his brothers and Jacob have tried to "pursue peace" (Hebrews 12:14a) with one another? List your ideas below:

   a. Joseph -

   b. Joseph's brothers -

   c. Jacob -

2. Have you ever tried any of the suggestions you listed above with someone with whom you were having difficulty? How did your efforts work out? Explain.

3. Despite our best efforts, in reality, it is only through the power of God's Holy Spirit that relationships are cleansed and restored. If we go back to Hebrews 12:14, we are told to first pursue peace and then holiness. I see this as a twofold process. First, we are to go to the person (Matthew 18) and, if for some reason you cannot restore peace, then you are to pursue personal holiness. Now, I am not describing pious, self-righteous "holiness." Rather, I am suggesting "Be holy, as I am holy" (1 Peter 1:16) kind of holiness; Christ's holiness. What practical ways can you be holy even in a situation when you cannot restore peace in a relationship?

4. If we do not try to pursue peace and holiness, the conclusion to Hebrews 12:14 tells us we may "fall short of the grace of God." What does it mean to fall short of the grace of God? How does bitterness and unforgiveness demonstrate falling short of the grace of God?

D **DELIGHTING** in God's Word

From today's verses, how has the Lord prompted you to pray?

Write a verse from the chapter that God has spoken to your heart.

Close in Prayer

WEEK 2

TRIUMPH OVER TEMPTATION

Genesis 39

His stomach likely growled as a reminder that He had not eaten in 40 days. But hunger was not the only thing intensifying; so was the spiritual warfare. Satan, a shameless opportunist, decided this was a promising moment to try and tempt Jesus. Perhaps he thought, "Surely, He is hungry, let me see if He will succumb to the temptation to fulfill His physical appetite." So, Satan said to Jesus, "If You are the Son of God, command that these stones become bread." But Jesus replied, "It is written, 'Man shall not live by bread alone, but by every word that proceeds from the mouth of God.' " Satan's first attempt to get Jesus to yield to the temptation he offered was unsuccessful, but Satan, being a tormenter, didn't give up that easily. He took Jesus up onto the pinnacle of the temple in Jerusalem to try another approach to tempting Jesus. This time Satan tried to use scripture against Jesus by saying, "If you are the Son of God, throw Yourself down. For it is written: 'He shall give His angels charge over you,' and 'In their hands they shall bear you up, lest you dash your foot against a stone.' " Jesus said to him, "It is written again, You shall not tempt the LORD your God." This underhanded move by Satan also proved to be a failure. Then the devil took Jesus up on a high mountain and showed Him the kingdoms around Him saying, "All these things I will give to You if You will fall down and worship me." Then Jesus said to him, "Away with you, Satan! For it is written, 'You shall worship the LORD your God, and Him only shall you serve.' Then the devil left Him, and behold, angels came and ministered to Him." (Excerpts taken from Matthew 4:1-11.)

Satan is described in the Bible as a liar, a roaring lion who wants to devour, a thief who is cunning as well as a murderer. With that list of rotten character qualities, it's no wonder he tried to tempt Jesus through many sly schemes! Satan tempted Jesus, the Son of God, in areas which are common to everyone, but He resisted the lust of the eyes (physical food), the lust of the flesh (physical body) and the pride of life (physical possessions). Not once do we see even the slightest hint of hesitation to consider the empty offers extended to Him by Satan. Further, Jesus demonstrated how we should fight the enemy by quoting back scriptural answers for every temptation. Jesus employed the words of James 4:7 which reminds us to "resist the devil and he will flee from you."

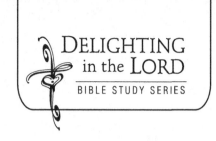

Today in our text, Joseph is presented with his own set of relentless temptations and, like Christ, Joseph did not give in to temptation. We will read how, as a high-ranking officer within Potiphar's home, he will gain the unwanted attention of Potiphar's wife. She will pursue him without any restraint in the hopes of having him indulge in sexual sin with her. But, this handsome, young man will not give in to the temptation no matter how alluring it might appear. Joseph stands strong in the face of Satan's plot to devour him. Temptations abound in our daily lives, and we must know how to resist them as well as our enemy. May we be found steadfast and immovable even when the most tempting circumstances arise, knowing that our text today gives us the courage to be triumphant in times of temptation.

RECEIVING God's Word

Open in Prayer
Read Genesis 39:1-23

EXPERIENCING God's Word

1. According to Genesis 39:1, Joseph has been bought by Potiphar, Pharaoh's personal security guard as well as an official in Egypt's government. Read Genesis 39:1-6 and list all the words describing God's favor to Joseph as well as to Potiphar.

   a. Read Genesis 12:1-3. How has God fulfilled his promise to Abraham through Joseph?

b.   From Genesis 39:1-6 how did God directly bless Joseph and Potiphar?

2.   Read Genesis 39:6-7. The Bible rarely mentions a person's physical traits. How is Joseph described physically and what effect did this have on Potiphar's wife?

3.   Read Proverbs 23:27-28. Here a harlot is described. How does Potiphar's wife fit this description?

4.   Scripture tells us in James 1:13 that temptation does not come by God. 2 Corinthians 11:3 says that Satan is the deceiver and deceived Eve by his craftiness. Potiphar's wife tried to tempt Joseph to sin using the schemes of the enemy. Based on Genesis 39:7-18, how was Potiphar's wife:

   • Persistent?

   • Enticing?

   • Seductive?

   • Forceful?

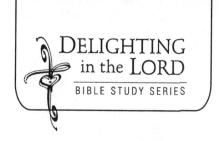

5. Read 1 Corinthians 10:13. Write the verse below.

6. Read Genesis 39:8-12. How did Joseph employ the strategies of 1 Corinthians 10:13?

   a. How did God make a way of escape for Joseph from the temptation of Potiphar's wife?

7. Read Psalm 51:1-4. Genesis 39:9 applies these Godly truths. In this verse, Joseph makes a statement to Potiphar's wife about why he cannot do what she is asking. How does his response speak to his faith and the truth about sin's effect?

8. Read Genesis 39:13-18. How does Potiphar's wife falsely accuse her husband, Joseph and her guards? Next to each false accusation write the truth for it.

9. In Genesis 39:19-20, Potiphar learns of his wife's accusations against Joseph. How does Potiphar respond to the accusations? How does Joseph respond?

> "If he [Potiphar] had really believed his wife's story, he probably would have had Joseph killed. As it was, he merely placed him in prison – a special prison 'where the king's prisoners were confined (v.20)'." (James Montgomery Boice, *Genesis Volume 3 Living By Faith*, pg. 935)

10. In Genesis 39:21 Joseph is now in prison. This is the second time he has watched his dreams seemingly die. Remember, he had a dream of being in a position of authority, but instead he was thrown in a pit and sold into slavery. Now he is a prisoner after spending eleven years rising to a position of prominence. What was it that sustained him in this difficult and discouraging situation?

11. Read Ephesians 6:5-8. Over the last two chapters we have very little written record of Joseph's response to his trials. What we do see is a steadfast faith in God. How was Joseph a bondservant as described in Ephesians 6:5-8? How was Joseph's steadfastness tied to God?

12. Read Genesis 39:22-23. Joseph's godly character impacts others once again, and God blesses Joseph while in prison. How does God bring about this blessing and what is it?

   a. In these verses, how does God demonstrate his abiding care and presence to Joseph?

13. Describe how you see God's sovereignty working in Joseph's life to this point.

TIME STAMP

Before the digital age, when important paper documents were received, a clerk would use an ink stamp to mark the time and date on them to stand as an official record of an event. It has been said that life events can also be like "time stamps" upon our hearts. Incidents that happen in life, both good and bad, leave an indelible stamp upon us and are not easily forgotten.

Joseph has many "time stamp" moments in his life. As you look back on this week's lesson, what events would you say are "time stamp" moments for Joseph?

A ACTING on God's Word

From the beginning of time, the devil has tried to mess with God's people causing them to shrink back in their faith, disobey God, and fall into full blown sin. If he can't keep people out of God's kingdom, he works to keep them useless for God's kingdom. One of his strategies is enticing people to sin through the lust of their eyes, the lust of their flesh and the pride of life (1 John 2:16). It started in the Garden of Eden with Adam and Eve. They lived in beautiful surroundings, had every need filled by God, and had a perfect relationship with Him. It was bliss. And then the enemy slithered his way onto the scene enticing Eve to sin.

The one tree God told Adam and Eve not to eat from is the one tree Satan used to tempt Eve. The enemy first downplayed their need for obedience and then denied the consequences God had given to Eve as a warning. He then enticed her with the beauty of the fruit, speaking of how it would satisfy all her desires. We all probably know the story in Genesis 3. The temptation overpowered Eve as she succumbed to her selfish desires. She took the fruit from the Tree of the Knowledge of Good and Evil, ate it and passed it to her husband, who joined her in the sin. God was true to His Word, as He always is. The consequences were devastating and far reaching, extending out to everyone born after Adam and Eve, including us. Adam and Eve's sin put God's redemptive plan in motion. He would send His Son, Jesus Christ, into the world to save sinners from the wrath of God and give eternal life through His death and resurrection to all who would believe in Jesus by faith.

1. Romans 3:23 tells us that we are all sinners. "For all have sinned and fall short of the glory of God." Today, we saw Joseph stand strong in the Lord in the midst of persistent and enticing temptation. Joseph knew that if he participated in Potiphar's wife's temptation he would be sinning before His holy and righteous God. He called sin, sin. Why is this important in temptation?

a. How does the enemy often downplay sin in our lives, trying to deceive us into believing sin isn't a big deal? How is this effective when he is tempting us?

2. Sexual temptations are pervasive and persistent in our culture today. Do you agree with this statement? Why or why not?

a. How does the enemy use sexual temptations in the lives of women?

3. Joseph said no to temptation. We can too. Saying no to temptation comes through the power of the Holy Spirit and our relationship with God through Jesus Christ. Sin is a heart issue as much as an obedience issue. Explain this. How can you overcome temptation through Jesus Christ?

If you've never received Jesus Christ into your heart by faith, you do not have the Holy Spirit empowering you in the area of temptation and sin. Today you can receive Jesus into your heart by faith. Romans 10:9-10 tells us that "if you confess with your mouth the Lord Jesus and believe in your heart that God raised Him from the dead you will be saved. For with the heart one believes unto righteousness and with the mouth confession is made unto salvation." Turn to the "Delighting In Your Salvation" page found at the beginning of this workbook and follow the steps given.

D DELIGHTING in God's Word

From today's verses, how has the Lord prompted you to pray?

Write a verse from the chapter that God has spoken to your heart.

Close in Prayer

DELIGHTING
in the LORD
BIBLE STUDY SERIES

WEEK 3

TRIUMPH IN GOD'S TIMING

Genesis 40 - 41:36

Much had happened in the preceding days. It was a whirlwind of sorts for Jesus' disciples. Just 40 days prior, Jesus was brutally crucified and hung on a cross for all of Jerusalem to witness his humiliation and death. As grief and confusion swirled in the heads and hearts of Jesus' followers, three days later Jesus would show himself alive to His disciples. It was all making sense. Jesus must suffer first and then His glory would come. The disciples began understanding the things Jesus shared while they had walked with Him witnessing miracles, signs and wonders; hearing His teachings, and perceiving but not understanding the things of which Jesus spoke. Now it was all coming together.

Jesus joined them in an upper room in Jerusalem. They had been waiting for Jesus to set up His kingdom on the earth. Would that time be now? Jesus told them that they were to continue waiting for the Promise of the Father to be fulfilled. The Holy Spirit was coming to empower them in a few days. The disciples got excited thinking the future was finally lining up with what had been promised in the past. They probed deeper into Jesus' heart anxiously asking, "Lord, will You at this time restore the kingdom to Israel?" Jesus interrupted their thoughts telling them, "It is not for you to know times or seasons which the Father has put in His own authority" (Acts 1:6-7). Jesus had work for His disciples to accomplish. He would use them to reach out into the nations with the truth of the Gospel, affecting lives for eternity. They weren't to be concerned with dates, times or seasons. They were to trust God and rely on Him to accomplish all that He had promised.

We see this very principle operating in Joseph's life as we study through our verses today. Joseph had been given a dream by God concerning his future. So many things didn't make sense as Joseph watched time and time again his life's trajectory change in unpleasant and unwarranted directions. But deep in his heart Joseph knew that God had His hand on each detail. As Jesus came to do the will of His Father in Heaven, so too, Joseph was doing God's will. His life was being used by God to touch the lives of rulers, jailers and prisoners in Egypt. As Joseph suffered much the last ten plus years, today we'll see Joseph brought to a place of status and glory with one man's suggestion. God is setting in motion the framework for Joseph to help save the Egyptians and Jews from starvation while pointing them all to God. Right where Joseph is, is right where God needs him to be.

Joseph could have easily lost heart, cursed God and fallen into despair; yet, quite the opposite is seen. His life demonstrates a deep conviction of God's love and sovereignty, allowing Joseph to truly triumph in God's timing. Waiting is so excruciatingly hard sometimes, especially when our eyes tell one story and our faith tells another. And yet, I (Stacy) have seen God's faithfulness over and over again in my life, my circumstances, my disappointments and my deep trials. I don't know what dreams God has put in your heart, but may you be encouraged as you study through the verses today that God's timing is truly best. "For the vision is yet for an appointed time; But at the end it will speak, and it will not lie. Though it tarries, wait for it; because it will surely come, It will not tarry." Habakkuk 2:3

R RECEIVING God's Word

Open in Prayer
Read Genesis 40-41:36

E EXPERIENCING God's Word

Experience 1: Genesis 40:1-23

1. Read Genesis 40:1-4. While in prison, Joseph meets two high-ranking men from the royal court who have been detained in the same prison as him. Who are they and what did they do to deserve being put in jail?

   a. What was Joseph's position of authority over these men?

2. Read Genesis 40:5-7. What new character trait is revealed through Joseph's behaviors toward the new prisoners when he saw they were sad?

3. In verse 8 we learn why the prisoners are sad. What is the reason given?

   a. Joseph responds to their need by acknowledging God's omniscience. How does he offer to help them?

   b. Read Jeremiah 17:7. Joseph has been in one trial after another for the last ten years, yet we see him speak confidently about the Lord and His power. What does this demonstrate about Joseph's faith in God?

   c. Consider that Joseph's dreams from God have not yet been realized, and his life circumstances do not demonstrate any likelihood that they will be fulfilled anytime soon. How might the enemy have used these circumstances negatively in Joseph's attitude, faith and willingness to listen to the butler's and baker's dreams?

4. In verses 9-11 the chief butler tells his dream to Joseph. Describe the dream in your own words.

5. Describe Joseph's interpretation found in verses 12-13.

6. Read Genesis 40:14-15. These verses seem to indicate that Joseph knew the butler had a direct connection to Pharaoh, who could release him from prison. How does Joseph solicit help from the butler and how does he explain his innocence?

7. Read verses 16 and 17. Explain in your own words the dream of the chief baker.

8. In verses 18-19 Joseph gives an interpretation of the baker's dream. What is it?

9. Read Genesis 40:20-23. Joseph's interpretations were proven correct. The chief baker was hanged, and the chief butler was restored. We are told in verse 23 that Joseph's request was not honored right away, and the chief butler forgot about him. How does this speak to God's providential care over Joseph and his trials?

   a. Even when circumstances look bleak, remember God is still in control over all things. Read the following verses and note what you learn about God's sovereignty.

      • Jeremiah 32:27 –

      • Job 9:5-10 –

      • Isaiah 55:8 –

      • Job 10:8-12 –

> "Joseph was bold enough to give an interpretation that could be proved right or wrong within three days. In only three days, everyone knew if Joseph was correct or not." (David Guzik, *Blue Letter Bible Commentary*, Genesis 40.)

Experience 2: Genesis 41:1-36

1. Read Genesis 41:1-8 and 17-24. Two years have passed and Joseph is still in prison. Pharaoh had two dreams that greatly troubled him. From the verses you just read, answer the question below.

Describe Pharaoh's first dream as it coincides with the image below.

Describe Pharaoh's second dream and draw your own picture of the content in the box below.

2. Read Genesis 41:9-15. The chief butler speaks to Pharaoh recounting his days in prison under the care of Joseph. Romans 8:28 says that "And we know that all things work together for good for those who love God, to those who are the called according to His purpose." In one moment, God changed Joseph's life situation for good. From these verses in Genesis, how did God use the people listed below to change the direction of Joseph's life?

   • Pharaoh

   • the magicians

   • the chief butler

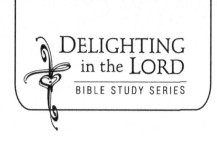

3. Read Genesis 41:16. What do you see in Joseph's answer to Pharaoh that gives God glory?

4. We now pick up the story in Genesis 41:25-32. These verses are Joseph's interpretation of Pharaoh's dream. In verse 25 Joseph tells Pharaoh that both dreams have the same meaning. What is it?

5. Read Genesis 41:33-36. How does Joseph appeal to Pharaoh after he interprets the dream and how does this open up the door for Joseph's initial dreams to be realized?

6. Describe how you see God's sovereignty working in Joseph's life to this point.

TIME STAMP

Before the digital age, when important paper documents were received, a clerk would use an ink stamp to mark the time and date on them to stand as an official record of an event. It has been said that life events can also be like "time stamps" upon our hearts. Incidents that happen in life, both good and bad, leave an indelible stamp upon us and are not easily forgotten.

Joseph has many "time stamp" moments in his life. As you look back on this week's lesson, what events would you say are "time stamp" moments for Joseph?

A ACTING on God's Word

Have you ever experienced a difficult time which tested your patience regarding God's timing only to encounter a person who repeated a well known cliché to try and encourage you? Perhaps they said something like, "God's ways are not our ways," or "God is rarely early, but never late." Although these statements are certainly true, often in times of waiting and uncertainty we just want answers sooner rather than later.

Stacy and I (Brenda) had planned to go away and write this study at a particular time, but "God's ways are not our ways." Stacy broke her leg, and then my husband had to be out of town when we were planning to be away, so we postponed our trip. We were both annoyed by the delay. Then a week prior to leaving on our rescheduled writing trip, I got the flu and a sinus infection. Once again, we needed to delay leaving until I was well enough to travel. "God is rarely early, but never late."

The funny thing though about the clichés I've mentioned is that they are actually pretty profound when coupled with the bigger picture of God's sovereignty. Stacy and I watched several interesting events unfold during the rescheduled trip, and they made us ponder God's timing. The day when we arrived to write, the internet was not working at the home where we were staying. The gracious homeowner reached out to the internet provider, and we received a technical support call from a gentleman in the Philippines. As he was trouble shooting, he began a conversation with us. He asked us if we were on a vacation. We explained we were not, but rather away to write a women's Bible study. He laughed and said, "You can pray for me." Well, you just know Stacy and I jumped on the chance to pray with the guy! We said, "Absolutely! How can we pray for you?" He told us that his wife was about to have their second child, and he wanted prayer for the birth of the child and her pregnancy. There was concern in his voice. He did not go into detail regarding the circumstances, just that he was expecting a baby girl. Before we concluded our call, Stacy and I prayed for him, his wife and the unborn child.

Stacy and I had an agenda when going away to write, and it included having working wifi, no distractions and lots of productivity! This unwanted glitch seemed like just another pause in accomplishing our purposes for the trip. However, after studying the life of Joseph for several days, we then saw our postponements as God's providential timing. We were given an opportunity to pray with a man who needed it, at just the right time, which might not have occurred if we had traveled to write as originally scheduled. Perhaps you can identify well with disturbances and delays. Let's take some time to reflect on how these may be used very purposefully by the Lord.

1. How do the following clichés about God's timing ring true in your life?
    You may provide your own cliché if you would prefer.

    • "God's ways are not our ways…"

• "God's rarely early, but never late…"

2. What Biblical principles apply to what you have written above? Is there a verse God has given you or a concept He is teaching you while you wait?

3. Now, let's get a bit more specific. Over the course of just the last month, write several delays that have unfolded. Then answer the questions below:

   a. Has God allowed you to see the purpose for the interruption(s)?

b. If He hasn't given you that level of clarity yet, write a prayer below thanking Him for what He will do with this set of events He has allowed and how it will strengthen your faith to trust His timing.

c. Is there anything in the lesson about Joseph's life that you can apply to your own waiting?

D **DELIGHTING** in God's Word

From today's verses, how has the Lord prompted you to pray?

Write a verse from the chapter that God has spoken to your heart.

Close in Prayer

DELIGHTING
in the LORD
BIBLE STUDY SERIES

WEEK 4

TRIUMPH OVER BETRAYAL

Genesis 41:37 - 42:38

Evening fell over Jerusalem as Jews throughout the city solemnly began to partake in the Passover meal. This was a yearly feast which served to remind the people how God saved the Israelites' firstborn sons from death when they were slaves in Egypt (Exodus 12). Jesus and his twelve disciples were among the locals who had gathered in an upper room to honor this celebration. This Passover meal would be unique from all others, because Jesus knew His time on earth was drawing to a close and there were many things He wanted to tell the men who were closest to Him. However, Jesus, troubled in His Spirit, knew a betrayer sat at the table with Him. The time had finally come to expose the traitor, a disciple named Judas. How it must have broken Christ's heart to look around at men He trusted and loved dearly, knowing that one of them did not have the same love and trust for Him in return. He knew the evil plan Judas had engaged in with the religious leadership. Judas somehow justified in his heart that a pitiful thirty pieces of silver in exchange for his friend, leader, and Savior was worth it.

Isaiah 53:3 prophetically tells us that He, (Jesus, the coming Messiah), was a man well acquainted with sorrows who understood grief. There are all types of sorrow and grief; however, betrayal can be a living grief which follows us relentlessly through life. Joseph understood this concept because he also was betrayed. Joseph's brothers, who should have desired to protect their younger brother, conspired against him. Today we will read in Genesis 42:21 that Joseph even pleaded with them for his life from the pit, but they refused to even acknowledge him. After selling Joseph to a caravan of Ishmaelites for a measly twenty shekels of silver, one must wonder what went through Joseph's mind as his traitors faded into the distance with each step he took toward Egypt. Betrayal must have been at the top of his list.

When loyalties are broken, scars are left on both the betrayed and the betrayer. This was certainly the case with Joseph and his brothers. Their motives for selling Joseph may have been fueled by jealousy and selfishness, but the next twenty years were spent with guilty consciences that hung around their necks like a noose. By the grace of God Joseph was eventually able to begin to heal from his wounds, unlike his brothers. Today we will see where the past begins to collide with the present as the betrayers meet up with the betrayed.

We must always remember that God is omniscient. He sees all and promises to make every wrong right, at some point, either now or in the life to come. If you have ever experienced the heartache of a broken allegiance, I (Brenda) pray you are given special encouragement from the Lord today through the story of Joseph's life. You are not unseen nor was your sorrow. God saw it and He alone will set things right.

RECEIVING God's Word

Open in Prayer
Read Genesis 41:37-57 and 42:1-38

EXPERIENCING God's Word

Experience 1: Seven Years of Plenty — Genesis 41:37-52

1. Read Genesis 41:37-41. What were the characteristics that Pharaoh saw in Joseph that made him choose him as second in command?

2. Read Genesis 41:42-45. Describe how Joseph was once again publicly revered. How is this similar to how his father had publicly honored him in Genesis 37?

> "Jewish legends say each letter of Joseph's Egyptian name means something. Linking them all together, the name is 'Seer-redeemer-prophet-supporter-interpreter of dreams-clever-discreet-wise.' More likely the name means 'God Speaks and He Lives,' referring to God's word coming through Joseph, his own preservation, and the way he has preserved the country." Dave Guzik, commentary on Genesis, *Enduring Word*, Blue Letter Bible.

3. In Genesis 41:46-49 we learn that Egypt is in seven years of abundance agriculturally. According to Pharaoh's dream, after seven years of plenty a famine would come next. According to these verses, how did Joseph prepare the country of Egypt for what he believed God was going to allow in a few years?

4. Joseph becomes a father in verses 50-52. Look at the names given to Joseph's sons. What healing has God begun in Joseph's heart in regard to his past?

5. It had been 13 years since Joseph had been stripped of his inheritance, sold as a slave, and taken to a foreign land where he was imprisoned. From these verses, how did Joseph's life fulfill Ephesians 3:20 thus far?

Experience 2: Seven Years of Famine — Genesis 41:53 - 42:24

1. A famine has taken over Egypt as was interpreted from Pharaoh's dream. Read Genesis 41:53-57. Describe the effect of the famine and Joseph's role in helping the people.

2. Read Genesis 42:1-8 and answer the following questions:

   a. In verses 1-2, Jacob commands his sons to go to Egypt to buy food in order to save the family from starvation. They seem reluctant. We are told that at the mere mention of the word Egypt, the brothers all looked at each other. What can you infer from this?

   b. How is Joseph's dream from Genesis 37 becoming a reality?

   c. Which brother was left behind with Jacob and why?

   d. How did Joseph react when he saw his brothers?

3. Joseph now remembers his dream from over 20 years ago. In Genesis 42:9 Joseph falsely accuses his brothers of being spies. Commentators have many suggestions for why he did this. Draw your own conclusion based on what you've learned so far.

4. How do the brothers both defend and describe themselves to Joseph in verses 10-13?

5. Joseph puts his brothers to the test by requiring them to prove their need for food. Read Genesis 42:14-20. List all the ways that Joseph's treatment of his brothers mirrored their previous treatment of him.

6. Read Genesis 42:21-24. What is still haunting the brothers and motivating their actions? How does this affect Joseph and the image he portrays to his brothers?

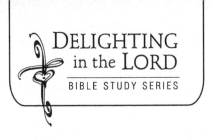

Experience 3: The Return to Canaan — Genesis 42:25-38

1. In Genesis 42:25-35 we learn that Joseph sends nine of his brothers back to Canaan with the intent for them to bring back Benjamin. In verse 28, one of the brothers sees that money has been put in his sack and he is afraid. Upon arriving in Canaan, they tell Jacob, their father, what happened in Egypt. They must bring back Benjamin in order to free Simeon from prison. Now they see each sack has their money inside. They are all afraid. Why is the money a point of fear for them and who do they blame?

2. In Genesis 42:36-38 we see Jacob and Reuben respond to the need for Benjamin to be brought back to Egypt. Describe both of their responses.

   Jacob -

   Reuben -

3. How do you see the sovereignty of God operating in these verses today?

TIME STAMP

Before the digital age, when important paper documents were received, a clerk would use an ink stamp to mark the time and date on them to stand as an official record of an event. It has been said that life events can also be like "time stamps" upon our hearts. Incidents that happen in life, both good and bad, leave an indelible stamp upon us and are not easily forgotten.

Joseph has many "time stamp" moments in his life. As you look back on this week's lesson, what events would you say are "time stamp" moments for Joseph?

A ACTING on God's Word

"For it is not an enemy who reproaches me; then I could bear it.
Nor is it one who hates me who has exalted himself against me;
then I could hide from him.
But it was you, a man my equal, my companion and my acquaintance.
We took sweet counsel together and
walked to the house of God in the throng." Psalm 55:12-14

Betrayal is at the very heart of our study in Joseph's life in the verses we studied today. Chances are, we've all experienced betrayal at some point in our lives. I (Stacy) have been betrayed by someone very close in my family. It's one thing to be betrayed by an enemy, but quite another when that person is someone who says they love you and shares life with you in one form or another. Betrayal from anyone hurts deeply and often leaves a gaping wound of pain and confusion.

Sometimes that wound heals over time, but if another betrayal or offense occurs, it's like someone has ripped the scab off the wound. Betrayal must be addressed in the heart of the believer, or it will become toxic and affect not only our relationship with God but also our relationships with others. Let's look at what we learned from Joseph's response to his betrayal and apply it to our hearts as we desire to triumph over betrayal.

1. Betrayal can cause us to respond in many different ways. Put a check next to the ways you see yourself responding when someone betrays you.

    ___ Defend my rights or position

    ___ Replay the events over and over again in my head

    ___ Try to get even

    ___ Speak poorly about the person who wronged me

    ___ Stew in silence

    ___ Harbor unforgiveness

    ___ Stay stuck in the pain caused

    ___ Shut people out/isolate

    ___ Ignore the betrayal

2. In today's verses we learned that Joseph had two sons named Manasseh and Ephraim. People's names in Scripture often hold great significance. The names of Joseph's two sons mean forgetful and fruitful. Let's look at Manasseh first. We are told in Genesis 41:51-52 that Joseph says Manasseh means "God made him forget all his toil and all his father's house." Let's look at how this word can be applied to betrayal.

    a. When betrayal occurs, why is forgetting so difficult?

b. How does the enemy use our inability to forget against us so we cannot move forward?

c. When Joseph says that God made him forget the troubles that happened in his father's house, he is saying that God has enabled him to forget his past. How is this possible and why is it essential?

d. Paul said in Philippians 3:13, "Brethren, I do not count myself to have apprehended; but one thing I do, forgetting those things which are behind and reaching forward to those things which are ahead, I press toward the goal for the prize of the upward call of God in Christ Jesus." How does this verse help us regarding betrayal?

3. Forgiveness is the key to God's enabling power to forget the wrongs done against us. We will look at this more throughout this study. Forgiveness is a decision to fully release a person of wrongdoing. Our greatest example of forgiveness is through Jesus Christ. Colossians 3:13 says, "as the Lord has forgiven you, so you also must forgive." Ephesians 4:32 says, "Be kind and compassionate to one another, forgiving each other, just as in Christ God forgave you." Forgiveness flows from our relationship with God. What is the direct command given to us by God and how is this possible?

4. Lastly, Joseph's second son was named Ephraim meaning, "God has caused me to be fruitful in the land of my affliction." It was God who healed Joseph's wounds and, for this, Joseph rejoiced and experienced fruitfulness. How does forgiveness from the heart bring fruitfulness in our lives and relationship with Jesus Christ?

5. End by reviewing your checked list from above and bring each area you checked before the Lord. Ask Him to first forgive you for these attitudes and behaviors, and then help you to forgive, forget, and be fruitful.

D **DELIGHTING** in God's Word

From today's verses, how has the Lord prompted you to pray?

Write a verse from the chapter that God has spoken to your heart.

Close in Prayer

WEEK 5

TRIUMPH IN GRACE

Genesis 43 - 44:17

It was the early morning hours. The sun was just coming up over Jerusalem as Jesus stood on the Mount of Olives taking in the scene around Him. The city was awakening and many Jews were making their way toward the Temple as the Feast of Tabernacles had concluded the day before. Jerusalem was bursting with people who had traveled there to celebrate. Jesus walked purposely toward the Temple as another day of teaching unfolded before Him. Just like the days before, people quickly gathered around Him, anxious to hear what He had to say. His words were always heart piercing, yet bathed in a love that was foreign to them. The crowd abruptly began separating as some of the scribes and Pharisees pushed their way through to Jesus with a woman being pulled closely behind. They placed her before Jesus declaring that she had been caught in the very act of adultery and, according to the Law of Moses, her punishment should be death. Anxious to trap Jesus and hear His judgment, they ask Him what He thought should be done with this woman. Would He excuse the sin or condemn her to death?

Jesus knew their tricks and traps. Even more, He knew their wicked hearts as well as the sin of this adulteress woman. Jesus couldn't be trapped. He reached down to write something in the dust. Angered that their question was ignored, the Jewish leaders asked again. Jesus raised his head asking for the person who is without sin to cast the first stone against this woman. He reached down again writing something in the dusty ground. Each person's heart was pricked as conviction flooded in and sin's guilt rose up. One by one their stones fell to the ground with a thud as old and young alike pulled away from the scene. The once large crowd was now an audience of one. Jesus, raising Himself from the ground and looking into the eyes of the adulteress woman standing before Him, asked her, "Woman, where are those accusers of yours? Has no one condemned you?" She responded, "No one, Lord." Tenderly looking at her, Jesus says, "Neither do I condemn you; go and sin no more" (John 8:10-11).

Overcome with the love and grace bestowed on her by Jesus, the woman turned to leave. Her guilt vanished, her life saved, and freedom given. She didn't deserve any of it, but that's what Jesus does; He gives the undeserving, repentant sinner forgiveness and eternal life.

Today we will see Joseph's brothers realize the only way to free their brother Simeon from the Egyptian jail is to return to Egypt, and bring their youngest brother, Benjamin, to Joseph. Knowing their father would be greatly troubled by this, they head back to Egypt regardless. Years of sin, guilt, and fear must have weighed down their hearts. Just like Jesus didn't punish the woman caught in sin, Joseph didn't execute punishment against his brothers. Instead, Joseph reached out with love, mercy, and grace toward his brothers. Many commentators will say that great heart change and transformation took place in the lives of Jacob, Judah and his nine brothers in these chapters. We'll let you examine the text for yourself and draw your own conclusions. What we will see are eleven men absolved of sin's penalty and given what they don't deserve as grace triumphs.

R RECEIVING God's Word

Open in Prayer
Read Genesis 43 and 44:1-17

E EXPERIENCING God's Word

Experience 1: Genesis 43:1-34

1. Read Genesis 43:1-5. What dilemma is before Jacob and his sons, and how is this a motivation for action?

2. Jacob (Israel) gets into a conversation with his sons regarding their current situation. Read Genesis 43:6-14 and answer the following questions:

a. Jacob and his sons are upset in verses 6-7. They are upset for different reasons. What are those reasons?

b. In verses 8-10 Judah makes a suggestion. What is his answer to the trouble they are facing and how is his response different from how he has acted in the past? (See also Genesis 37:26-28.)

c. Jacob makes the final decision in verses 11-12. He realizes there is only one way for Simeon to return home and his family to be saved. What is his solution?

d. In verses 13-14 Jacob has a change of heart. Describe what that is and what might have caused this change. Include words or phrases from the verses that helped draw that conclusion.

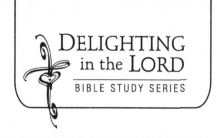

> When Abram's name was changed to Abraham, the old name was never used again; the new name represented a profound and permanent growth in his character. It has been otherwise with Jacob. His name was changed to Israel at Jabbok, but it is not often after this that his new or covenant name is used. Usually, he was thinking and operating much as the old Jacob had done. He was self-centered, self-serving, complaining. However, at this point of the story we see Jacob emerging as Israel, as a 'prince with [or 'one who has been conquered by'] God.' In this character he rightly appeals to the sovereign God (God Almighty) for the issues outcome."
> (James Montgomery Boice, *Genesis Volume 3 – Living by Faith*, p. 1025)

3. Read verses 15-17. The traveling distance between Canaan and Egypt is about 250 miles which would have been a three-week trip. In verse 15 the brothers arrive in Egypt and go before Joseph. In verses 16-17, when Joseph sees his brothers returning, what does he tell the steward to do in order to receive them?

4. Read verses 18-22. We are told "the men were afraid" upon entering Joseph's house. Why are they afraid and how do they defend themselves?

5. Read verses 23-25. The steward responds with Godly character. How does his response demonstrate the following attributes?

    a. Peace

    b. Mercy

    c. Grace

6. When Joseph first encountered his brothers back in Genesis 42:7, we were told he spoke roughly to them. Read Genesis 43:26-34. Describe the many ways Joseph behaves very differently in this encounter.

7. This is an opinion question and there is no correct answer. Why do you think Joseph has not revealed his identity to his brothers by now?

Experience 2: Genesis 44:1-17

1. Read Genesis 44:1-3. What things did Joseph tell his steward to put in the brothers' sacks?

2. In verses 4-13 it seems that Joseph has set a trap for his brothers. Describe his actions and what he may have been trying to accomplish.

   a. Compare the brothers' responses in Genesis 42:21-22 with Genesis 44:10-13.

3. Read Genesis 44:14-17. In these verses there are parallels between Joseph's actions toward his brothers and the way Christ extends grace to us. Read the quotes on the left. Then look up the verses on the right and describe the connection you see.

GENESIS 44:14-17	VERSES
"his brothers came to Joseph's house" (v.14)	Matthew 11:28-30
"and they fell before him" (v.14)	James 4:10
"what deed is this you have done?" (v.15)	Romans 3:23
"Judah said, "What shall we say to my lord?" (v.16)	Romans 10:9
"Or how shall we clear ourselves?" (v. 16)	John 3:16-17
"God has found out the iniquity of your servants;" (v. 16)	1 John 1:9
"here we are, my lord's slaves, both we and he also with whom the cup was found." (v. 16)	Romans 6:6-7
"And as for you, go up in peace to your father." (v. 17)	John 14:27

TIME STAMP

Before the digital age, when important paper documents were received, a clerk would use an ink stamp to mark the time and date on them to stand as an official record of an event. It has been said that life events can also be like "time stamps" upon our hearts. Incidents that happen in life, both good and bad, leave an indelible stamp upon us and are not easily forgotten.

Joseph has many "time stamp" moments in his life. As you look back on this week's lesson, what events would you say are "time stamp" moments for Joseph?

A ACTING on God's Word

The word grace is used in the Bible to express the unmerited favor of God extended toward us. In Genesis 44 we see Joseph extend grace to his brothers many times. Whether it was when Joseph was welcoming the brothers into his home, releasing Simeon from prison, or providing them with a meal, Joseph repeatedly demonstrates unmerited kindness toward his brothers. Joseph knew that his brothers did not deserve his lavish grace, yet he chose to extend it.

1. Does extending grace mean we should ignore a sin done against us? Why or why not?

2. Is genuine grace ever hard to extend? Why or why not?

3. Ephesians 2:8-9 says this, "For by grace you have been saved through faith, and that not of yourselves; it is the gift of God, not of works, lest anyone should boast." As a born-again believer in Jesus Christ, you have accepted Christ's free gift of grace to cover your sin. How does this knowledge help you extend grace to others?

4. Is there a situation or a person that needs to be covered in grace that you have not been willing to lavish upon them? Pray now and ask God for a fresh perspective upon the situation or person, coupled with the ability to see it with the eyes of grace. If God gives you direction during your time of prayer with actions you are to take, write them below.

D DELIGHTING in God's Word

From today's verses, how has the Lord prompted you to pray?

Write a verse from the chapter that God has spoken to your heart.

Close in Prayer

"The one thing I ask of the Lord - the thing I seek most - is to live in the house of the Lord all the days of my life, delighting in the Lord's perfections and meditating in his temple." Psalm 27:4

DELIGHTING
in the LORD
BIBLE STUDY SERIES

WEEK 6

TRIUMPH IN FORGIVENESS AND RECONCILIATION

Genesis 44:18 - 45:28

Jesus was just finishing up a time of prayer with His heavenly Father when one of His disciples approached Him and asked if He would teach them to pray. The model prayer Jesus recited for them is likely one of the most well-known prayers in the entirety of the Bible. The Lord's Prayer, found in both Matthew 6:9-13 and Luke 11:2-4, says this:

> *"Our Father in heaven,*
> *Hallowed be Your name.*
> *Your kingdom come.*
> *Your will be done*
> *On earth as it is in heaven.*
> *Give us this day our daily bread.*
> *And forgive us our debts,*
> *As we forgive our debtors.*
> *And do not lead us into temptation,*
> *But deliver us from the evil one.*
> *For Yours is the kingdom and the power*
> *and the glory forever. Amen."*

One of the aspects which Jesus included in His prayer was the importance of forgiveness. We are to forgive as we have been forgiven. At the conclusion of His prayer, He felt the need to give even more instruction on the topic of forgiveness by saying, "For if you forgive men their trespasses, your heavenly Father will also forgive you. But if you do not forgive men their trespasses, neither will your Father forgive your trespasses." Certainly, conviction must have fallen upon some of Jesus' listeners. Jesus wanted His disciples to understand how critical it is to forgive. In just a short period of time, He was about to demonstrate the ultimate act of forgiveness by allowing Himself to be crucified in order to forgive the sins of mankind. If He, who was without sin, could forgive us, how much more should we be able to do the same for others? Further, Jesus' sacrifice on the cross would make it possible for humanity to be reconciled back to God, because our sins were paid for once and for all.

Joseph's life emulates the kind of forgiveness Jesus both taught and demonstrated. Joseph chose to forgive his brothers for the offenses they had committed against him. He chose not to hold onto unforgiveness. This pleased God and He honored Joseph's exoneration with a beautiful family reconciliation which will unfold in our story today. May God convict us as needed if we are holding unforgiveness. May we be quick to forgive, knowing it is necessary as a believer in Jesus. May we experience the freedom which comes from forgiving. May we be blessed with reconciliation with those we have forgiven.

RECEIVING God's Word

Open in Prayer
Read Genesis 44:18-34 and 45:1-28

EXPERIENCING God's Word

Experience 1: Genesis 44:18-34

1. Read Genesis 44:18-34. Judah is pleading with Joseph over the detainment of his brother Benjamin. In his pleas, he uses many tactics to try and get Joseph to relent which would allow Benjamin to go back home to Canaan. Look at the list of tactics Judah used and match the statements on the left with the verses on the right where you find this tactic being used.

Judah's personal responsibility	v. 33-34
Appealing to Joseph's authority	v. 19,23, 32
Appealing to his previous honesty to Joseph	v. 32
Judah's personal sacrifice	v. 18
Judah's humility toward Joseph	v. 24-31
Sympathy for Jacob, Benjamin's father	v. 19-23

2. Last week we witnessed a change in Judah when he told Jacob he would protect Benjamin to and from Egypt. In verses 18-34 Joseph is witnessing a changed Judah. How is Judah different from how Joseph probably remembered him?

Experience 2: Genesis 45:1-28

1. Read Genesis 45:1. Why does Joseph finally decide to reveal himself to his brothers?

2. In Genesis 45:2 Joseph has a deeply emotional response. Describe it.

3. Read Genesis 45:3-4. What is the first question Joseph asks after revealing his identity? What does this demonstrate about his deepest concern?

   a. Joseph's brothers are speechless in verse 3 when they hear "I am Joseph." Imagine for a minute what must have been going through their heads. Write your thoughts below.

> The word "dismayed" in Genesis 45:3 means to disturb, alarm, terrify, hurry, be disturbed, be anxious, be afraid, be hurried, be nervous. (www.blueletterbible.com, Strong's Hebrew Lexicon H926 - bahal. Genesis 45)

b. In verse 4 what does Joseph do to reassure his brothers? Why might they need reassuring?

4. After Joseph tells his brothers he is Joseph, he reminds them of what they did to him previously. Read Genesis 45:5-8. Notice the first two words in the beginning of verse 5: "but now." The word *but* cancels out what was said before it and signals something important is coming next. Here we see Joseph give a very gracious response to his brothers' previous mistreatment. Who does he credit with the decision to send him to Egypt?

a. We know that God is not the author of evil. Explain Joseph's response within this truth. Read Job 1:6-12 for further understanding on evil and God.

b. List the three reasons Joseph believes he was sent to Egypt.

c. Explain how Joseph's response is an example of forgiveness and reconciliation.

5. Read 2 Corinthians 5:18-21. We are told that we have been reconciled to God through Jesus Christ, and that we have been given the ministry of reconciliation as ambassadors for Christ as though God were pleading through us. How was Joseph an example of this as an Old Testament believer?

6. Joseph is very concerned about his father, Jacob. He immediately tells his brothers to go home and share the good news with their father. Read Genesis 45:9-13. What are the reassurances that Joseph tells his brothers to share with Jacob?

   a. What command does Joseph give his brothers in verse 13?

7. What does the emotional but genuine response seen in Genesis 45:14-15 say about the relationship now between Joseph and his brothers?

8. Read Genesis 45:16-20. Describe Pharaoh's generosity toward Joseph and his family.

9. Joseph prepares his brothers to return to Canaan to get his father. Read Genesis 45:21-23. What items does Joseph give to his brothers prior to their departure? Why do you think they are significant? Notice the differences.

10. Verse 24 is so insightful. Even though many years have passed and hurts have been forgiven, Joseph appears to still think previous behaviors might emerge. What advice does Joseph give as they depart?

11. In Genesis 45:25-28 the brothers leave Egypt and head back to Canaan to share their good news with Jacob. How did Jacob respond to the news that his son Joseph was still alive and in a position of prominence in Egypt?

    a. Why do you think he initially had trouble believing what the sons were sharing? What made him finally receive their news as truth?

TIME STAMP

Before the digital age, when important paper documents were received, a clerk would use an ink stamp to mark the time and date on them to stand as an official record of an event. It has been said that life events can also be like "time stamps" upon our hearts. Incidents that happen in life, both good and bad, leave an indelible stamp upon us and are not easily forgotten.

Joseph has many "time stamp" moments in his life. As you look back on this week's lesson, what events would you say are "time stamp" moments for Joseph?

A ACTING on God's Word

Forgiveness:
-To grant a pardon for an offense, cease to feel resentment against an offender, and/or cancel a debt against another person

1. Joseph understood that all that happened to him was allowed by God. With this understanding, he was able to more easily forgive his brothers. How does our focus on God instead of focusing on who is wrong or right help in our ability to forgive someone who has wronged us?

2. Forgiveness is both modeled and commanded by God. It was modeled for us in the life, death, and resurrection of Jesus Christ for the sins of the world. And in Matthew 6:14-15 we see it commanded to us. "For if you forgive men their trespasses, your heavenly Father will also forgive you. But if you do not forgive men their trespasses, neither will your Father forgive your trespasses." Our desire and ability to forgive someone who has hurt or wronged us flows first out of our relationship with Christ. How is forgiveness an act of love and obedience?

3. Does forgiveness condone or endorse another person's wrongdoing? Explain.

4. Is there someone in your life who needs your forgiveness today? Can you identify why you haven't forgiven him or her? What is holding you back from extending this forgiveness?

Reconciliation:
-to win over to friendliness, bring into agreement or harmony; restore to favor settling differences

1. In today's verses we saw Joseph exhibit forgiveness and reconciliation with his brothers. Reconciliation happened after Joseph saw an undeniable change in his brother Judah's heart. Explain the difference between forgiveness and reconciliation. Can one happen without the other? Explain.

D DELIGHTING in God's Word

From today's verses, how has the Lord prompted you to pray?

Write a verse from the chapter that God has spoken to your heart.

Close in Prayer

WEEK 7

TRIUMPH IN GOD'S FAITHFULNESS

Genesis 46 - 47

It had been a brutal few days. As Sunday dawned in Jerusalem, those who loved Jesus were still mourning his death. It was only three days ago that they were watching Jesus suffer an excruciating death as His body was nailed to a cross and hung for all to see. Their Messiah was dead. Confusion intermingled with grief flooded their minds. Little did they know that a day of mourning would quickly turn to joy.

Mary Magdalene, Mary the mother of James, and Salome made their way to Jesus' tomb early that Sunday morning. They were anxious to anoint Jesus' body with spices. The sun was rising as earthquake tremors shook the ground. It didn't stop them. They approached the tomb but, to their astonishment, the stone had been rolled away. Sitting on the stone was a man clothed in white, glowing like the sun which was beginning to shine in the distance. He knew why they were there and immediately comforted them. "Do not be afraid, for I know that you seek Jesus who was crucified. He is not here; for He is risen" (Matthew 28:5-6a). The women entered the tomb and saw it was empty. Jesus' body was gone. The angel of the Lord said to them, "Remember how He spoke to you when He was still in Galilee, saying, 'The Son of Man must be delivered into the hands of sinful men, and be crucified, and the third day rise again.' " (Luke 24:6-7) And Jesus' words came flooding back to their hearts. He is alive just like He promised. The women ran to tell the disciples the great news.

That evening, the disciples gathered together in Jerusalem. Fear permeated the air in the room. They knew the Jewish leaders were seething with anger over Jesus' resurrection and the accusations that might come their way. They were still processing all that occurred that day. The one they loved was dead, yet now was alive. How could this be? The next thing they knew, Jesus was standing in their midst, showing them His hands and His side, and calming their fears saying, "Peace to you!" (John 20:21) What a glorious day it was; Jesus was reunited with His disciples and would very soon return to His Father in glory, just as He said He would.

For the disciples, it was only a three-day waiting period from Jesus' death to His resurrection. For Jacob, it had been 22 long years believing that his son Joseph was dead before learning the truth. In our verses today we will see Jacob reunited with his beloved son, Joseph. It's hard enough when we don't see someone we love very often. But imagine believing someone is dead, then several years later finding out they are alive. What a reunion it would be!

Not only will Joseph welcome his family into Egypt during a time of great famine, but God will use Joseph and all of the circumstances of the past 22 years to provide for the children of Israel as God continues to set up His promised Jewish nation. God chose Joseph to save the children of Israel during a time of great famine and despair. God would also use Joseph to provide for their needs and bring them blessings, as He remains faithful to His promises going all the way back to Abraham.

Hebrews 13:8 tells us that "Jesus is the same yesterday, today and forever." He is faithful. Sometimes as we wait on God's promises to be fulfilled, we can grow weary and allow doubt to creep into our hearts. Maybe you find yourself in this place today? And yet, just as Jesus met the disciples in the upper room bringing them peace, Joseph meets his father and brothers bringing them peace. Their needs would be met, their well-being sustained, and their lives blessed in ways they couldn't even imagine. From Egypt to Jerusalem to your life today, God is faithful to meet you in your need, bringing peace where there is fear and directing your steps according to His will for your life.

RECEIVING God's Word

Open in Prayer
Read Genesis 46-47

EXPERIENCING God's Word

Experience 1: Genesis 46

1. Read Genesis 46:1. Recall, Israel is Jacob. Jacob journeys to Egypt with his family to see Joseph. What does he take with him? What does this signify about his travel plans?

2. In verse 1 we learn that as Jacob journeys, he makes a stop along the way. Where did Jacob go?

   a. This place holds great significance in the lives of Jacob's grandfather, Abraham, and his father, Isaac. Read the verses below and describe the importance of this location.

   • Abraham: Genesis 21:22-34

   • Isaac: Genesis 26:23-33

3. In Genesis 46:1 we are told that Jacob offered sacrifices to God. Consider why he chose to do this. What might have been his reasons?

   a. What do his actions signify about his heart's attitude toward God?

4. In Genesis 46:2-4 God speaks to Jacob. How does God reassure Jacob?

a. Think about what is happening. Jacob is leaving the land of God's promise and going to a foreign land. Why might he need reassurance?

5. In Genesis 46:1-4 we see Jacob referred to as both Jacob and Israel. In Week 5 of our study you read about Jacob's name being changed to Israel. You may go back and read the text box if you desire. When God changes a name, He often refers to the person by their new name going forward. This has not been the case with Jacob as seen in our verses today. He is referred by both his new and old name. Why might this be significant?

6. Read Genesis 46:5-7. Jacob and his entire family are leaving Canaan and going to Egypt. How did God provide for this journey?

a. How does this demonstrate God's faithfulness?

7. In Genesis 46:8-27 we are given the names of the 12 tribes of Israel who went with Jacob to Egypt. This is the first time the Israelites are referred to as the children of Israel. Verse 27 tells us there were 70 persons in the house of Jacob. This number does not include the wives of Jacob's sons. This was a large group of people traveling together. The family genealogy listed below is from these verses.

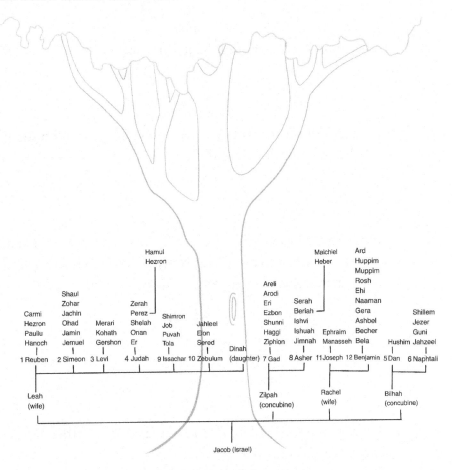

Family Tree designed by Rebecca Harris.
The number beside each son's name indicates birth order.

a. Why did God give both Jews and Gentiles this record? How does this demonstrate God's faithfulness to His people?

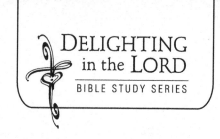

b. Think about God's promise to Abraham and Isaac regarding the nation of Israel. How has God used Joseph to establish the nation and further fulfill his promise?

8. In Genesis 46:28, who led the journey to Joseph?

   a. Look at the family tree on the previous page. Who should have led the group based on birth position?

   b. Re-read Genesis 37:26-28. Why may it have been significant that Judah was sent out first to meet Joseph when they entered Egypt? Can you think of any other reasons why Judah may have been in the lead?

9. In Genesis 46:29-30 Joseph is reunited with his father. It has been 22 years since Jacob last saw Joseph. Describe the reunion.

> "Jacob was satisfied to see his son alive, for he was the one designated as the heir, the one whom God had chosen to rule over the family. So, this was more than a family reunion; it was a confirmation that God's promised blessing was intact." (*Bible Knowledge Commentary*, Old Testament, p. 95)

10. Joseph has a plan to provide for his family during the famine as well as keep them close to him. Read Genesis 46:31-34. How do you see Joseph's wisdom and leadership demonstrated in his plan?

Experience 2: Genesis 47

1. Read Genesis 47:1-4. How do Joseph and his five brothers express respect and submission to Pharaoh when they meet him?

2. According to verses 5-6, how does Pharaoh's response exhibit his respect and admiration for Joseph, considering shepherds were an "abomination" in the Egyptian culture?

3. Read Genesis 47:7. When Pharaoh meets Jacob, Jacob does something unusual. Read Hebrews 7:7. How does this verse speak into the exchange between Jacob and Pharaoh?

4. Read Genesis 47:8-10. How does Jacob describe his life to Pharaoh?

a. How was this significant considering he thought his son Joseph was dead for the last 22 years?

5. In the provisions God has given through Joseph in Genesis 47:11-12, what promises were fulfilled from Genesis 12:1-3?

6. Back in Genesis 41, Pharaoh had a dream about the years of plenty and the years of famine, and at that time he appointed Joseph as governor over the land and the people. Read Genesis 47:13-26. In this role, God uses Joseph to provide for Pharaoh and the people.

   a. How does God use Joseph to save the people when there was:

   • No bread? (v.13)

   • No money? (v. 15)

   • Nothing left? (v. 18)

   b. How does God use Joseph to bless Pharaoh through the famine?

   c. In verse 22, whose land was not bought by Joseph and why?

d. In these verses Joseph does not profit personally; instead, we see him acting graciously toward both the people and Pharaoh. Explain.

7. Based on Genesis 47:13-26, how is Joseph's relationship with the Egyptians like Jesus' relationship with believers?

8. Read Genesis 47:27-31 and answer the following questions:

a. From verse 27, describe what life looked like for Jacob and the nation of Israel as they lived in Egypt.

b. As Jacob's life is drawing to a close, he has a final request of Joseph. What is it?

c. Jacob and Joseph make a covenant with each other. How is this demonstrated?

d. Why would Jacob not want to be buried in Egypt?

9. How has God been faithful to Jacob for 147 years?

10. How do you see God's sovereignty in Genesis 46 and 47?

TIME STAMP

Before the digital age, when important paper documents were received, a clerk would use an ink stamp to mark the time and date on them to stand as an official record of an event. It has been said that life events can also be like "time stamps" upon our hearts. Incidents that happen in life, both good and bad, leave an indelible stamp upon us and are not easily forgotten.

Joseph has many "time stamp" moments in his life. As you look back on this week's lesson, what events would you say are "time stamp" moments for Joseph?

A ACTING on God's Word

Genesis 46 begins with an encounter between Jacob and God. This is not the first time Jacob has interacted with God. You may recall their interaction previously in Genesis 32:22-31. In verse 28 Jacob was given the name Israel after he struggled with God. "And He said, *'Your name shall no longer be called Jacob, but Israel; for you have struggled with God and with men, and have prevailed.'* "

This was a tenuous time in Jacob's life. He was leaving his uncle's service and returning to his homeland where his estranged brother, Esau, lived. This was likely a highly stressful time in his life and full of questions without known answers. Questions like: Would his brother be willing to forgive him? Could he find a new place to live and provide for his family? Could he maintain peace with Esau, even if he did not kill him immediately upon his return? But God assured and blessed Jacob in a time of his deep unrest and trouble. And just as God was faithful in Genesis 32, He would be faithful again many decades later in Genesis 46.

In our text today we found Jacob again needing reassurance from God. Jacob was once again moving his family, but this time from Canaan to Egypt. True to God's faithful character, He met Jacob in his time of distress and anxiety. To prepare him for the days ahead, God reminded him of some powerful truths about His character. We read four specific encouragements in Genesis 46:3-4 from God to Jacob:

> I am in control: "I am God" (v. 3)
>
> I give peace: "Do not fear" (v.3)
>
> I give direction and blessing: "Go down to Egypt, for I will make of you a great nation there" (v.4)
>
> I am with you: "I will go down with you" (v. 4)

These reassuring words spoken to Jacob of God's faithfulness should be an encouragement to us today as well, because we know God never changes. Therefore, what He did for Jacob, He can also do for us. Just as God was faithful to Jacob, He will be faithful to us even when He asks us to walk through circumstances we may not understand.

1. Are you facing something that is causing you unrest? If so, what is it?

2. Re-read the four encouraging statements from Genesis 46:3-4 listed below. Then complete the prayers that are started for you. Express how you will trust God in the circumstances which are causing you unrest.

- "I am God" (v.3)
  Dear God, because you alone are God, therefore I will...

- "Do not fear" (v. 3)
  Lord, thank you that I do not have to fear. Please help me...

- "Go down to Egypt, for I will make of you a great nation there" (v.4)
  Holy Spirit, you give perfect direction and You know just what blessings to bestow upon me. As I follow your direction...

- "I will go down with you" (v. 4)
  Jesus, you tell me that you will never leave me nor forsake me. Please help me...

3. Praise the Lord in your heart for what He will do now and in the days ahead as you watch Him be faithful to you, just as He was to Jacob.

 DELIGHTING in God's Word

From today's verses, how has the Lord prompted you to pray?

Write a verse from the chapter that God has spoken to your heart.

Close in Prayer

WEEK 8

TRIUMPH IN GOD'S BLESSING

Genesis 48 - 49

The day described for us in Mark 10 likely unfolded as so many other days. Jesus was teaching the multitudes who came to listen to His wisdom which was unparalleled to anything they had heard elsewhere. The crowds gathered around Him and, as was His custom, He taught them. The lesson of the day was not recorded for us; however, Jesus did something highly unusual which impacted both the parents and the children in the audience. Mark 10:13 states that people brought their children to Jesus so He might touch them. This was a strange request because children were considered too insignificant to bother someone like Jesus. However, when Jesus saw His disciples' response, He was greatly displeased. He said to them, "Let the little children come to Me, and do not forbid them; for such is the kingdom of God. Assuredly, I say to you, whoever does not receive the kingdom of God as a little child will by no means enter it. And He took them up into His arms, laid His hands on them and blessed them." (Mark 10:14-16) Can you imagine for a moment what it looked like for the One who created that child to then speak blessing over that same child? Now that is a one-of-a-kind baby dedication service!

Jesus was a man full of compassion, so He must have known the parents present desired for their precious children to be held by the Messiah. Jesus graciously and lovingly took their children into His arms and blessed them. I (Brenda) can only imagine what Jesus said that day since it was not recorded in the Bible. I wonder, did He tell what future events were to come for the children, including both the joys and trials they would endure? Did He speak words of encouragement to the hearts of the children's parents, so they could cling to His words in the days ahead? Did He divinely warn the children or their parents of things they should avoid as well as what to embrace? Whatever was actually spoken by Jesus that day, it must have been profound.

In Genesis 48 and 49, we will get a glimpse into a different but similarly profound moment in Old Testament Biblical history. Jacob, nearing his death, will bless some of his sons and two of his chosen grandchildren. Jacob's words will be prophetic, holding deep significance for not only the future of his sons but also for the nation of Israel. He will give warnings, corrections, commendations, and blessings. Some of the sons will receive very little, or no blessing at all, while Joseph will receive a double blessing. Jacob's favoritism was still evident even after 147 years.

I am so grateful that Jesus doesn't have favorites. Unlike earthly fathers, our heavenly Father convicts, forgives, and blesses His children with perfect, unconditional love. He does not hold a grudge nor unforgiveness toward His children. He desires to give them hope and a future, as well as to bless and make them a blessing. There is triumph in God's blessing. His children have an eternal inheritance that never corrupts nor fades away. Take a few moments to thank God for this truth before you begin your study in Genesis today.

RECEIVING God's Word

Open in Prayer
Read: Genesis 48 and 49

EXPERIENCING God's Word

Experience 1: Genesis 48

1. Read Genesis 48:1-4. Jacob is coming to the end of his life and is sick. He has three very important points he desires to make with Joseph before he dies. The first has to do with God's promise to him and the future of Israel. Joseph brings his two sons, Manasseh and Ephraim, to Jacob. Jacob repeats a promise to Joseph which he received from the Lord years previously, as recorded in Genesis 28:10-22. List the promises that Jacob recalls from God below.

2. The second of the three points that Jacob wanted to convey to Joseph was regarding past sins of his sons and their future effect on Israel as a nation. A little bit of prior knowledge is needed in order to understand Jacob's actions. In Genesis 35:22 Reuben had sexual relations with Jacob's concubine Bilhah. This brought lifelong consequences which are recorded in 1 Chronicles 5:1. In Genesis 34 Simeon and Levi take revenge on Shechem and his people for raping their sister. Jacob was infuriated with all three of these sons for their actions and lack of restraint. As a result, Jacob does something very unusual in Genesis 48:5-6. Read these verses and explain what you learn.

3. The third of the three points Jacob makes to Joseph is regarding his love for Joseph's mother. Read Genesis 48:7. What does Jacob recall?

Jacob, by adopting Joseph's two sons, Ephraim and Manasseh, as his own (are mine), and thus elevating them to a position equal with his other sons, insured that Joseph's descendants would receive a double inheritance. Apparently at this time Jacob transferred the rights of the firstborn from Reuben to Joseph, the firstborn of his beloved Rachel (cf. vv. 15-16; 1 Chron. 5:1). (*KJV Ryrie Study Bible*, pg. 81-82)

4. In Genesis 48:8-9 Jacob asks Joseph to bring his two sons to him, so they may be given a blessing. What stands out to you in the way Joseph describes his two sons?

5. Read Genesis 48:10-12. Describe how Jacob (Israel) receives his two grandchildren, and how he says God has blessed him.

6. In Genesis 48:13-14 Jacob (Israel) knowingly places his hands on each boy's head. What does he do and what consequences would result for the boys?

7. Read Genesis 48:15-16. Jacob's blessing could be broken into three parts. In these verses there is prayer, adoption and blessing of great posterity. Write the verses that correspond with the headings below:

Prayer —

Adoption —

Blessing of great posterity —

a. Do you see any connections between this blessing and what occurs when a person makes a confession of faith in Christ? Explain.

b. In verses 15-16 Jacob describes God in three ways. How does Jacob describe Him and what does this say about his faith?

8. In Genesis 48:17-18 Joseph becomes upset with his father. Why?

9. Read Genesis 48:19-20. Here we see Jacob is adamant about the reversal of the blessing. Fill in the verse below with Jacob's response to Joseph:

Verse 19a (NKJV) "But his father refused and said, "I _____, my son, I_____.

a. In verse 19 the word "know" in Hebrew is Yada' (H3045) which means *to perceive or to know with intimate knowledge*. How does this explanation impact your understanding of what Jacob is saying to Joseph prophetically?

b. Read Numbers 1:32-35. How do you see Jacob's prophecy fulfilled over 400 years later?

This [prophecy] was fulfilled in Israel's history. Both tribes were blessed, but Ephraim was greater as a tribe, even to the point where the name Ephraim was used to refer to the whole northern nation of Israel (see examples in Isaiah 7:8, 7:17, and 11:13). (David Guzik, BlueLetterBible.com)

10. Read Genesis 48:21-22. Jacob leaves Joseph with some final words of reassurance. What are they? From all you have learned from Jacob's life thus far, describe how these words speak about his deepening faith and trust over the years.

Experience 2: Genesis 49

Read Genesis 49:1-2. On Jacob's death bed he calls his sons together to talk with them regarding their future. He speaks both as a prophet and a father. This is the first time in Scripture we read of a testimony and revelation as someone is nearing the end of life. The prophecies and blessings we will be examining in this chapter are not only personal to Jacob's sons, but also extend to the future generations of Israel as well.

Below we have listed each son/tribe. Jacob's words to his sons reveal the future, warn about the consequences of sin, encourage Godly living, and predict the coming Messiah, Jesus Christ. Read the verses that go with each son and fill in the headings, if they apply. If they do not apply, leave the heading blank. We will then have you look up the verses that testify to the prophetic fulfillment of Jacob's words.

1. **Reuben:**

   Read Genesis 49:3-4

   Reveal future:

   Warn of consequences of sin:

   Encourage Godly living:

   Predict the coming Messiah:

   What is Reuben compared to? What does this comparison mean?

   Prophetic Fulfillment:

   1 Chronicles 5:1-2

   Matthew 19:30

2. **Simeon and Levi:**

   Read Genesis 49:5-7

   Reveal future:

   Warn of consequences of sin:

   Encourage Godly living:

   Predict the coming Messiah:

   What are Simeon and Levi compared to? What does this comparison mean?

   Prophetic Fulfillment:

   Joshua 19:1,9

   Compare Numbers 1:23 with Numbers 26:14

3. **Judah:**

   Read Genesis 49:8-12

   Please note Shiloh (H7886) means "Tranquil from H7951 – to be tranquil, to be secure. As well as, he who it is or that which belongs to him. So it means: He who brings tranquility." Shiloh is seen as a title of the Messiah.

   Reveal future:

Week 8: Triumph in God's Blessing

Warn of consequences of sin:

Encourage Godly living:

Predict the coming Messiah:

What is Judah compared to? What does this comparison mean?

Prophetic Fulfillment:
Deuteronomy 33:7

Numbers 24:17

Psalm 78:67-70

Revelation 5:5

From David until Herod, a prince of Judah was head over Israel (even Daniel in captivity). The promise was that Israel would keep this scepter until Shiloh comes. Even under their foreign masters during this period, Israel had a limited right to self-rule until 7AD. At that time, under Herod and under the Romans, their right to capital punishment – a small but remaining element of their self-governance – was taken away. At the time the rabbi's considered it a disaster of unfulfilled Scripture. Seemingly, the last vestige of the scepter had passed from Judah, and they did not see the Messiah. Reportedly, rabbis walked the streets of Jerusalem and said, 'Woe unto us, for the scepter has been taken away from Judah, and Shiloh has not come.' Yet God's word had not been broken. Certainly, Jesus was alive then. Perhaps this was the very year He was 12 years old and discussed God's Word in the temple with the scholars of His day. Perhaps He impressed them with His understanding of this very issue."
(David Guzik, BlueLetterBible.com)

4. **Zebulun**

Read Genesis 49:13

Reveal future:

Warn of consequences of sin:

Encourage Godly living:

Predict the coming Messiah:

What is Zebulun compared to and what does this comparison mean?

Prophetic Fulfillment:

There is no Scriptural reference to show this fulfillment. Alfred Edersheim, a well respected Biblical scholar, postulated this was fulfilled in 30 A.D. There are several guesses as to the "when" of this prophetic fulfillment.

5. **Issachar**

Read Genesis 49:14-15

Reveal future:

Warn of consequences of sin:

Encourage Godly living:

Predict the coming Messiah:

What is Issachar compared to? What does this comparison mean?

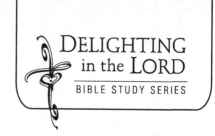

6. **Dan:**
Read Genesis 49:16-18

Reveal future:

Warn of consequences of sin:

Encourage Godly living:

Predict the coming Messiah:

What is Dan compared to? What does this comparison mean?

Prophetic Fulfillment:
Judges 18:27-31

7. **Gad:**
Read Genesis 49:19

Reveal future:

Warn of consequences of sin:

Encourage Godly living:

Predict the coming Messiah:

Prophetic Fulfillment:
Deuteronomy 33:20-21

8. **Asher:**
   Read Genesis 49:20

   Reveal future:

   Warn of consequences of sin:

   Encourage Godly living:

   Predict the coming Messiah:

   Prophetic Fulfillment:
   Deuteronomy 33:24-25

9. **Naphtali**
   Read Genesis 49:21

   Reveal future:

   Warn of consequences of sin:

   Encourage Godly living:

   Predict the coming Messiah:

   What is Naphtali compared to? What does this comparison mean?

   Prophetic Fulfillment:
   Deuteronomy 33:23

Week 8: Triumph in God's Blessing

10. **Joseph:**
Read Genesis 49:22-26

Reveal future:

Warn of consequences of sin:

Encourage Godly living:

Predict the coming Messiah:

What is Joseph compared to? What does this comparison mean?

Prophetic Fulfillment:
Deuteronomy 33:13-17

11. **Benjamin:**
Read Genesis 49:27

Reveal future:

Warn of consequences of sin:

Encourage Godly living:

Predict the coming Messiah:

What is Benjamin compared to? What does this comparison mean?

Prophetic Fulfillment:
Judges 19-21

12. Read Genesis 49:28-33. Describe Jacob's death and burial wishes.

13. Read Hebrews 11:21. Here Jacob's faith is remembered by his words of blessing recorded in Genesis 49. Why is this significant and what does this say about faith that endures?

14. From today's verses, what Biblical truths do you see between sin, God's blessing toward us, and our heart toward obedience?

15. How is God's grace seen in the blessings given to Jacob's sons?

TIME STAMP

Before the digital age, when important paper documents were received, a clerk would use an ink stamp to mark the time and date on them to stand as an official record of an event. It has been said that life events can also be like "time stamps" upon our hearts. Incidents that happen in life, both good and bad, leave an indelible stamp upon us and are not easily forgotten.

Joseph has many "time stamp" moments in his life. As you look back on this week's lesson, what events would you say are "time stamp" moments for Joseph?

A ACTING on God's Word

As a parent, I (Stacy) love blessing my kids. No matter their ages, I long to make their lives easier, help them be prosperous, and give them unexpected blessings along the way. But my desire to bless them is tempered by my desire for them to become mature, responsible adults, as I never want them to feel entitled or to lack personal responsibility. It is sometimes a difficult balance to achieve as a parent, because I love them so much. I want to give them all they need, yet also equip them to handle the things of life. Even when my children don't obey me or walk in obedience, my heart still wants to bless them because of my deep love for them.

1. In Matthew 7:11 Jesus said, "If you then, being evil, know how to give good gifts to your children, how much more will your Father who is in heaven give good things to those who ask Him?" We serve a God who loves us more than we can comprehend. He, too, longs to bless His children. But let's look at the word *blessed*. The very words, *to bless*, (H1288) means to cause to prosper; the result of divine favor; but it also means to make to kneel.

When we think of God's blessing, I think we often get confused at what His blessing is and what it should look like. Our minds so often long for the tangible things of life before the spiritual. Can you relate?

a. How would you define a blessing?

b. How would you define God's blessing?

c. What does it mean to you to live a "blessed" life?

2. In today's verses, Jacob, under the direction of the Holy Spirit, spoke blessings on his sons. Those blessings probably didn't make a lot of sense to his sons in the moment and may have even seemed troubling. Yet the blessings, as well as the prophecies, all had spiritual implications. The things Jacob spoke were not about possessions gained or status reached; they were about how Jacob's sons cooperated with God's eternal plan of salvation and how it would affect them.

a. Do you believe your blessings from God are contingent on your level of obedience to Him? Read James 1:25, Luke 11:28 and Matthew 6:26-34 to help you answer this question.

b. Read Ephesians 1:3 and Ephesians 2:8-9. What are the blessings God wants to give us? Have you done anything to deserve or increase God's blessings in your life? Explain.

3. In today's verses we saw Jacob bless Ephraim and Manasseh. Jacob prayed over them, and spoke of adoption and prosperity. Romans 8:14-17 speaks to these same points. It says, "For as many as are led by the Spirit of God, these are sons of God. For you did not receive the spirit of bondage again to fear, but you received the Spirit of adoption by whom we cry out, 'Abba, Father.' The Spirit Himself bears witness with our spirit that we are children of God, and if children, then heirs— heirs of God and joint heirs with Christ, if indeed we suffer with Him, that we may also be glorified together." Below are listed blessings from God taken from these verses. Explain how these are blessings for the believer. How are they blessings in your life?

a. Freedom

b. Intimacy

c. Inheritance

d. Assurance

e. Purpose

f. Suffering

4. Psalm 1:1-3 speaks of God's blessing to the believer.

    a. How is the one blessed defined in this verse?

    b. What is the object of their heart and what does their prosperity look like?

5. Make a list below of all the blessings that God has given you. Are there things in your life that at first didn't seem like a blessing, but you have come to see it that way? Explain. Take a moment to thank Him for the way He has blessed your life.

D   DELIGHTING in God's Word

From today's verses, how has the Lord prompted you to pray?

          Week 8: Triumph in God's Blessing

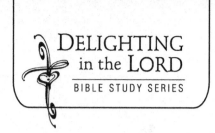

Write a verse from the chapter that God has spoken to your heart.

Close in Prayer

WEEK 9

TRIUMPH TO THE END

Genesis 50

They stood on Samaritan soil. Soil that usually went untouched by Jewish feet because the Samaritans were hated by the Jews and regarded as impure. But to Jesus, the Samaritans had the same needs as everyone else; they needed Him and the salvation that only He could give. While on their way to Jerusalem, Jesus brought His disciples through Samaria. Upon arriving, his disciples went on into the city to find lunch, but Jesus stayed behind at the city's well for a divine encounter with a woman living in sin. He knew she would come to the well that day. In the midst of her sin, loneliness, and desperation, He extended grace to her. She received what she had never been given before; freedom from her past and forgiveness moving forward. As this woman runs to the city to tell everyone about this man Jesus, the disciples meet up with Jesus and offer him lunch. Knowing He must have been hungry and tired, His disciples urged Jesus to eat. He refused and said, "My food is to do the will of Him who sent Me, and to finish His work." (John 4:34)

Jesus had one purpose given to Him by the will of His Father, God Almighty. He came to earth to save sinners. A purpose which would conclude in His horrific and painful death at the hands of the very people He came to save. God's purpose was always Jesus' focus despite the cost, the betrayal, the rejection, or the personal pain. The soil of Samaria wouldn't stop Him, the rejection from the Jews wouldn't stop Him, and even the cross wouldn't stop Him. 1 Peter 2:24 says, "[He] who Himself bore our sins in His own body on the tree, that we, having died to sins might live for righteousness – by whose stripes we are healed." Every day lived here on earth, Jesus lived to finish God's will for you and me (Stacy). As His body hung nailed to the cross and He knew all things were accomplished for the fulfillment of God's plan, He ushered up the triumphant words we all need to hear, "It is finished." (John 19:30) With that, Jesus took His last breath.

As we come to the last lesson of the study of Joseph, like Jesus, we see Joseph triumphing over evil to the end. Throughout the study, we've seen Joseph abandoned, rejected, accused, and imprisoned; events resulting from actions of the brothers he loved so dearly.

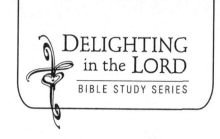

As we'll see today, the past sin of the brothers resurfaces in their hearts following the death of their father, Jacob. Fearing Joseph will now retaliate against them, they beg him for forgiveness. Joseph had already forgiven them years prior. Yet, Joseph will extend complete forgiveness again, receiving them with love and tenderness. They were forgiven and set free from the penalty of that sin. Joseph communicated God's grace. They needed to receive the grace given and walk in that freedom. And Joseph, triumphing in God, said, "You meant evil against me, but God meant it for good, in order to bring it about as it is this day, to save many people alive." (Genesis 50:20) Like Jesus does for us, Joseph bore the griefs of his brothers and carried their sorrow away, all the while he himself suffered affliction (Isaiah 53:4). Joseph's life speaks to a life of deep faith in God; faith that triumphs when circumstances speak of defeat. As God used Jesus' life to save those hopelessly lost in sin, so too, God used Joseph to save his father, his brothers, and a nation. From the evil intended, God raised Joseph up in power, protected his witness, gave him position and made him prosper. It is what He desires to do with us, too.

Joseph knew God was greater than any evil seen or circumstance experienced. Joseph knew God was in control of all things. His very words attest to his faith in God. God knows what He's doing even when our circumstances might declare otherwise. Joseph speaks with confident assurance as he responds to his brothers saying, "Am I in God's place?" (Genesis 50:19). For truly it is God, and God alone, who forgives, saves, and redeems.

As Joseph's life comes to an end on this side of heaven, he doesn't speak of his personal victory or triumph, but speaks of God's grace and faithfulness. He triumphs in God; who He is, His grace, His faithful promises, His eternal perspective, His greater good. It is those words he leaves with his brothers. "God will visit you, and bring you out of this land to the land of which He swore to Abraham, Isaac and to Jacob." (Genesis 50:24) God is with you. In that, and that alone, we can triumph to the end!

R RECEIVING God's Word

Open in Prayer
Read Genesis 50: 1-26

E EXPERIENCING God's Word

1. Read Genesis 50:1-3. Describe Joseph's emotional response to Jacob's death and the instructions on how to prepare Jacob's body.

> "Pharaoh commanded the Egyptians to observe an official mourning period for Jacob. After all, Jacob was the father of the second ruler in the land. This kind of recognition was usually reserved for important people like Pharaoh himself or members of his family. The forty days of the embalming period and the seventy days of the official mourning were probably concurrent." (W. Weirsbe, *Be Authentic*, p. 179)

2. In Genesis 50:4-9 Joseph goes to Pharaoh asking for permission to take the 300 mile journey to Canaan to bury his father. Pharaoh gives his permission. Describe the processional and include who went and who did not.

3. Read Genesis 50:10-11. Threshing floors were typically located outside the city in a large elevated place where many people could gather at one time. This is where Joseph chose to mourn Jacob publicly. What affect did this observance have upon the Canaanites?

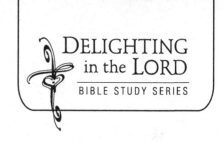

4. In Genesis 50:12-14 Jacob's body is laid to rest in the cave of the field of Machpelah. Why is this place significant?

5. Read Genesis 50:15-18. Despite many years of abundant provision and the demonstration of Joseph's forgiveness toward them, Joseph's brothers were fearful of him after coming back to Egypt. Why are they afraid and what does this say about their acceptance of Joseph's forgiveness all those years?

   a. Read Genesis 45:2-5 and compare it with Genesis 50:15-18. Why do you think Joseph responded to the request of his brothers and their actions with weeping?

   b. Read Genesis 42:6 and compare it with Genesis 50:18. Think about Joseph's dream back in Genesis 37. Draw some conclusions based on Joseph's dream, the first appearance of his brothers before him in Egypt, and their response now toward him as their brother. How do you see evidence of Joseph's dream being fulfilled?

6. Read Genesis 50:19-21. Verse 20 is one of the most quoted verses from this chapter. What do you learn from this verse about how God turns evil into good?

   a. Joseph demonstrates many attributes of the fruit of the Holy Spirit (love, joy, peace, patience, kindness, goodness, faithfulness, gentleness and self-control). Which one stands out the most to you from verses 19-21? Explain why you chose it.

7. Read Genesis 50:22-23 and Proverbs 17:6. How do you see this Proverb being fulfilled at the end of Joseph's life?

8. In Genesis 50:24 Joseph gives his brothers an encouragement similar to his father's. How does Joseph encourage his brothers?

9. Read Hebrews 11:22 and then read Genesis 50:25. What does this say about the depth of Joseph's trust in God and His promises?

10. Read Genesis 50:25-26 and then answer the following questions:

    a. From Genesis 50:25-26 what was Joseph's request? Read Exodus 13:19 and Joshua 24:32. Who fulfilled Joseph's request?

    b. According to Genesis 50:26, where does Joseph's body remain until his request is fulfilled?

11. Throughout the study we have looked at how Joseph is a type of Christ. His life was a foreshadowing of the Messiah. From what you learned, list all the ways you see Joseph resembling Christ throughout his life.

TIME STAMP

Before the digital age, when important paper documents were received, a clerk would use an ink stamp to mark the time and date on them to stand as an official record of an event. It has been said that life events can also be like "time stamps" upon our hearts. Incidents that happen in life, both good and bad, leave an indelible stamp upon us and are not easily forgotten.

Joseph has many "time stamp" moments in his life. As you look back on this week's lesson, what events would you say are "time stamp" moments for Joseph?

A ACTING on God's Word

"But as for you, you meant evil against me; but God meant it for good, in order to bring it about as it is this day, to save many people alive." Genesis 50:20

"Satan weaves; God reweaves" – Max Lucado

Perhaps one of the most well-known quotes about Joseph's life is found in Genesis 50:20. I (Brenda) believe it is so frequently quoted because it is relatable and reassuring. Evil things happen around us daily. We are witnesses to heartache, destruction, trouble and disasters, and they are disturbing. When evil seems to have the upper hand, both believers and non-believers can question God saying, "Why, God?" I know in my own life, there have been times I have asked this question of the Lord because I cannot see how my circumstances could possibly be "good." But, just because I cannot see the good to come does not mean it won't come, or that I will fully understand the "good" He is orchestrating. We must accept that there are things God, in His wisdom and mercy, allows us to see and things He chooses not to reveal to us. I heard an analogy which put a unique perspective on difficult events. There is an obvious size difference between a Saint Bernard and a no-see-um (sand flies). If you were camping and both a Saint Bernard and a sand fly were in your tent, you would certainly see one and likely not the other but, regardless, both were present. We can ask God to show us the "good" in difficult events but, in the end, we must trust He is at work, regardless if we ever witness the good He alone weaves into evil circumstances.

1. Have you ever watched the news only to learn about evil events and questioned, "Why, God?" If so, give an example.

2. How can both evil (Satan) and good (God) be working concurrently in the same situation?

3. Romans 8:28 says, "And we know that all things work together for good to those who love God, to those called according to His purpose." Knowing that this verse is true, how are you encouraged to trust God more with the things you cannot understand? How is this humbling?

4. How can you, like Joseph, respond to someone who meant to harm you with words similar to those found in Genesis 50:20? How can this verse help you to forgive more readily?

5. Look back through your study on Joseph. What chapter/lesson stood out to you the most and why? What have you learned from the life of Joseph about living a life of triumph?

a. What part of your walk has God been working on since the start of this study? What progress have you seen Him make as you've submitted to His authority over you in this area?

b. How would you summarize the study of "Joseph's life" in one or two sentences?

6. Throughout the study, you have noted circumstances in Joseph's life that probably were time stamped on his heart. These were difficult and often painful situations that changed the trajectory of his life. He probably remembered the details and the time of each event for many years. Time stamps in life can also come from joyous occasions. Think over your life and list the "time stamps" that you have mentally recorded, whether from a painful or joyous event/circumstance. How have you seen God use those "time stamps" in your life? Look over your list and detail God's sovereignty and faithfulness in using those events in your life for His glory.

D **DELIGHTING** in God's Word

From today's verses, how has the Lord prompted you to pray?

Write a verse from the chapter that God has spoken to your heart.

Close in Prayer

BIBLIOGRAPHY

Boice, James Montgomery. Genesis: *An Expositional Commentary*. Baker Books, 2006.

"Free Bible Commentary from Pastor David Guzik." *Enduring Word*, enduringword.com.

Radmacher, Earl D., et al. *Nelson's NKJV Study Bible: NKJV, New King James Version*. T. Nelson, 2007.

Ryrie, Charles Caldwell. *Ryrie Study Bible: King James Version*. Moody Press, 1994.

Strong, James. *The New Strong's Compact Bible Concordance*. Thomas Nelson Publishers, 2004.

Walvoord, John F., and Roy B. Zuck. *The Bible Knowledge Commentary: an Exposition of the Scriptures*. Victor, an Imprint of Cook Communications Ministries, 2004.

Wiersbe, Warren W. *Be Authentic: Exhibiting Real Faith in the Real World: OT Commentary, Genesis 25-50*. David C. Cook, 2010.

www.blueletterbible.com

Made in the USA
Middletown, DE
07 June 2022